A Historical Examination of Some Non-Markan Elements in Luke

A Historical Examination of Some Non-Markan Elements in Luke

By
ERNEST WILLIAM PARSONS, PH.D.

WIPF & STOCK · Eugene, Oregon

Wipf and Stock Publishers
199 W 8th Ave, Suite 3
Eugene, OR 97401

A Historical Examination of Some Non-Markan Elements of Luke
By Parsons, Ernest William
ISBN 13: 978-1-60608-754-1
Publication date 6/1/2009
Previously published by University of Chicago Press, 1914

TABLE OF CONTENTS

PAGE

INTRODUCTION. A Statement of the Purpose and Method of This Essay   9

I. AN EXAMINATION OF THE MATERIAL CONTAINED IN LUKE 9:51—18:14

    I. The General Missionary Interest 16

    II. The Samaritan Interest 24

    III. The Reciprocal Opposition of Pharisees and Christians . . 30

    IV. The Emphasis on Discipleship 34

    V. The Ascetic Interest 38

    VI. The Teaching on Exorcism 41

    VII. The Prayer Element 43

    VIII. The Miracle Element 46

    IX. The Christology 49

    X. The Progress of Christianity 54

    XI. Other Indications as to Time and Place 55

II. AN EXAMINATION OF THE NON-MARKAN MATERIAL CONTAINED IN LUKE, CHAPS. 3–8

    I. The Sermon on the Plain 63

    II. The Remainder of the Material 69

Grateful acknowledgment is made by the author of his indebtedness to all his instructors. He wishes especially to express his gratitude to Associate Professor Shirley Jackson Case, whose interest and counsel have stimulated and aided him in his task.

INTRODUCTION

The discovery and recognition of the practical or functional element in the writings of both Old and New Testaments have produced results of great value for the interpretation of these books. As long as the approach was from the standpoint of absolutism—that is, as long as the statements which the writings contained were considered valid and true *per se*, as well as authoritative and equally applicable to all time and to every conceivable circumstance—so long did formidable difficulties arise on almost every page the scholar examined. It is not claimed that the application of the principle of pragmatic interest has solved all the problems or laid all the specters, but it is contended that no scientific interpretation is possible where the immediate circumstances of the writing, with regard both to the writer and to those to whom the document was directed, are ignored.

A brief review of some of the New Testament writings will serve to illustrate and establish the position. The correspondence of Paul with the Corinthian church presents almost innumerable difficulties if an attempt is made to interpret it apart from a definite problem-situation. As long as the thought of universal validity was maintained the difficult passages, such as speaking with tongues, eating of meats, the suggestions regarding marriage, the conduct of women in public worship, either were passed by lightly, received fanciful explanations, or were rendered grotesque by an attempted application of them unchanged to the differing conditions of another age. The recognition of the definite purposes and aims of this correspondence not only has cleared up many perplexing statements, but has enhanced the religious value of the letters for modern life. The reality of the problems of that day, the primitive ideas, the crude yet splendid attempts at readjustment of old and new on the part of this church, as well as the sanity and insight of the great apostle, emerge with considerable clearness when viewed from the strictly historical side.

The strange atmosphere of the Colossian letter, especially in the sphere of christological thought and statement, is exceedingly difficult apart from a knowledge and recognition of the definite aim which the writer had before him. The differences between this letter and those generally acknowledged to be Pauline are so marked as to have occasioned grave questioning as to whether the apostle could have produced

it. The recognition of the incipient heresy with its peculiar characteristics against which the writer so stoutly contended has furnished the
key to the situation, and, although we may not know all we wish to know
concerning the sect at Colossae, enough is known to explain why the
theological thinking of the apostle manifests this rather sharp turn.

The Roman letter is but poorly understood until we remember the
bitter conflicts and bitterer experiences which had fallen to the lot of
the author while he labored in the East. His work practically completed there,[1] this missionary-statesman, with visions of western worlds
to conquer, in which campaign Rome as a base of operations was almost
indispensable, pens the document which is to introduce him to the church
in that city and forestall those opponents who hung upon him so tena-
ciously. Approached in this way, much of the letter becomes luminous.

Few, if any, of the books of the New Testament have given rise
to so many baffling questions, have suffered so many fantastic interpretations, as that which closes the Canon. The history of its interpretation is full of interest[2] but that is not our concern here. It was not until
indications of a definite situation were discovered and expressions which
disclosed the purpose of the writer in connection with this situation
were noted that any real progress in the comprehension of the Apocalypse
was made. If this book is read in the light of the Domitian persecution,
the rare faith and fine courage of the author bear a message which cannot
fail to be of effect.

The First Epistle of John is in danger of sad misunderstanding
unless it is recognized that it was written to combat certain errors which
the author considered serious. Hostility to Docetic Gnosticism which
was developing along the lines of aristocracy and libertinism was without doubt one of the determining factors in the composition of this
letter. Not to remember this and not to allow for it is to miss the
original meaning of its composer.

So far little exception will be taken to our statements. In fact
it would not be a difficult matter to show that all the epistolary literature of the New Testament was produced by problem-situations more
or less definite. But what of the gospels—those fountain-heads of our
knowledge of Jesus? Has the pressure of circumstances been operative
there? Do these gospels with their resemblances and differences arise
from definite situations which have determined their material and

[1] Rom. 15:23.

[2] See von Dobschütz, *The Eschatology of the Gospels*, pp. 39–60; H. B. Swete,
The Apocalypse of St. John, pp. cciii–ccxv; R. H. Charles, *Studies in the Apocalypse*.

colored its presentation to a greater or less degree? It is coming to be, if it is not already, generally recognized that this is true in a striking way of the Fourth Gospel. The points of dissonance and disagreement between it and the Synoptics are seen to be very largely the result of definite situations and aims which controlled its production. To take but one example: the representation of John the Baptist in the Fourth Gospel with its peculiar and striking dissimilarities to the Synoptic picture is wonderfully well explained as a polemic against a Johannine sect which preferred claims for its founder that made him a rival of the Christ.[1] It can scarcely be gainsaid that the Fourth Gospel is a pragmatic work, and in the light of this admitted fact it must be interpreted.[2]

As to the Synoptics, the answer is not so clear nor so unanimous. There have been statements as to the purposes of these gospels, but they are general purposes only and throw but little light on many of the problems. It is true that Luke gives a statement of purpose in his preface,[3] but it carries us only a short distance on our way. Of Mark some are content to say that he sets forth the public career of Jesus with little or no conscious argumentative purpose;[4] others, however, detect a more or less definite purpose. One is justified in saying that it was written for purposes of propaganda and not as critical history. With regard to Matthew it is generally said that his aim is to show that Jesus is the Old Testament Messiah founding the kingdom which after Jewish rejection is thrown open to all. Sometimes a definite situation is suggested, but rarely with assurance. It is in the very nature of things that there should be a greater amount of indefiniteness in discovering the exact purpose of the Synoptics, assuming for the moment that they have more than a general one. In the first place, the narrative and biographical material which they use serves at times to make the discovery of purpose difficult. The charm of the narrative diverts the attention and only by careful searching can such purpose be detected. In the second place, these writers are using for a later period stories of a past or passing generation, and sayings that ostensibly were spoken by a person of a past generation in view of situations which confronted him at the time of speaking. The matter is further complicated by the

[1] As to the existence of such a sect, cf. Acts 19:1-5, and p. 44.

[2] Note the specific aim of the Fourth Gospel as stated in 20:31. For a statement of the aims of the Fourth Gospel, cf. E. F. Scott, *The Fourth Gospel*, pp. 65-103; Baldensperger, *Der Prolog des vierten Evangeliums*.

[3] Luke 1:1-4.

[4] Cf. Ernest D. Burton, *A Short Introduction to the Gospels*, pp. 33-40.

use of sources which in all probability themselves took form in whole or in part in response to immediate needs in the early Christian communities. It is not required for the purposes of this essay to trace this matter farther here. The pragmatism of the Synoptics, while highly probable and generally admitted, is discoverable only after a patient and somewhat minute examination. But its discovery, even with what lack of definiteness may attach to it, has been of value and will be increasingly so in the determination of origin and date.

The point of the foregoing partial survey has been merely to show the existence, and that generally of a specific and definite purpose in the New Testament writings. They were not written merely because an author wished to produce. They did not aim—in nearly all cases—to be historical works, at least, primarily. They were rather writings pressed out in the heat of controversy, struck out by the blows of the militant young religion as it met its foes and thrust back its frontiers, and sometimes called forth by the pain and mystery of persecution. That is to say, they were produced in some definite historical situation and to meet some specific need which is reflected more or less clearly on their pages.

If the books of the New Testament as they now stand are found on examination to manifest practical aims which help in their interpretation and elucidation, is there any valid reason against carrying back the process to the sources of these books where such sources are discoverable? Will it not yield the same assistance in regard to these sources as it has yielded in regard to the books themselves? This has been done in a measure in the case of the Apocalypse. The remains of an older Jewish apocalypse, some Christian apocalyptic reflecting the time of Nero, and later additions from the time of Domitian, have been thought by some to be discoverable there. But we are in a better position in the matter of the discovery of sources with respect to the First and Third Gospels than with respect to any other books in the Canon. The use of Mark by each, the statement of Luke himself, and the comparison of the non-Markan sections of these gospels yield us results which cannot be obtained elsewhere in our field. There is no need to detail or even to outline the work that has been done on the literary relationships of the Synoptics. Our concern is not with that. The purpose of this essay is to submit some of the non-Markan material of the Third Gospel to an examination from the historical and problem-situation standpoints, with a view to discovering the interests which lay behind the formation of the tradition and thus to gain a knowledge of the provenance of such tradition and the date at which it probably took form.

Too often the approach to the study of the gospels is from the standpoint and the days of Jesus. This is done even by those who are investigating in a historical spirit and who are endeavoring by historical method to interpret the documents. Is there not at least as much to be said in favor of an approach from the standpoint of the Christian community in the period of gospel-making when these traditions were taking shape, or assuming new forms, either orally or in writing? Is it not strictly historical and psychologically correct to consider the gospel sources in the light of the pressing and insistent needs of the primitive Christian communities? It is incredible that the circumstances which caused the tradition to be preserved and emphasized should not color, and possibly determine, the selection and form of the products of their literary and pedagogical activity.

It is with the hypothesis that the problem-situation is a valuable touchstone for interpretation that the approach to this material is made. The method pursued will be to interrogate the various sections of the material with a view to discovering the purpose which it was designed to serve and to find the situation into which it fits with the greatest degree of probability. It is claimed that if certain sections manifest aptitude to serve certain purposes and such purposes which needed serving can be located in time and place we shall be justified in giving grave consideration to the possibility of those sections having arisen in oral or literary form at that time and in that location. Moreover, if a considerable number of sections show marked ability to function at a similar place and about the same period, and if we find this material existent in compact and solid form, it will be considered that there is a strong presumption in favor of considering this material either a document or a selection from a document. On the other hand, if in the course of our examination of the material certain sections of it should disclose such a diversity of problem-situations and characteristics as to call for a change of provenance, or if the controlling purposes appear to be essentially different, and if such diversity should continue in a fairly consistent way, it will be considered a valid argument for the differentiation of these sections into separate sources. This difference need not extend to every detail, for whatever the provenance or situation, there would of necessity be some common elements through community of general subject and aim.

Two matters call for consideration here. This discussion does not concern itself with the question of the historicity of the statements recorded in the material it considers. There will be little inclination to deny that our gospels are interpretations of Jesus—his person, teaching, and works. The fact that they are interpretations, even interpretations arising amid stress of special situations to meet which they assumed approximately their present form, does not of itself involve a departure from essential historicity. A reflective interpretation may be as accurate as an unreflective one. It may even be possible that a reflective interpretation may give a closer approximation to the real significance of the events.[1]

Neither does the literary aspect of the synoptic problem intimately concern us here. This study may have a bearing on that question, but it approaches the material unhampered by any theory. While this is true, it must be said that the two-document theory is assumed to be not proven. The second source, Q, is on the basis of that hypothesis assumed to be a document. Upon how precarious a foundation this assumption rests the various attempts which have been made to reconstruct it clearly show. Much work on the problem has been vitiated by too rigid an adherence to it. It is at least as probable, in view of the phenomena of the First and Third Gospels, that Matthew had sources independent of Luke, and vice versa, while these sources may have possessed common material. Is it not possible that in the crystallization of tradition common material may have found itself in juxtaposition with peculiar material? The possibility of the emergence of similar problem-situations in various places and at slightly different times must be considered in the attempt to explain the variations of Matthew and Luke. It is an assumption largely gratuitous that all the common material in Matthew and Luke must have come from the same immediate source. Our approach to the study of the non-Markan Luke will be unhampered by the question of its relation to Matthew. The material will be taken as it stands in Luke and examined by the method outlined above.

Those parts of the Third Gospel which will come under our consideration are: (1) that block of material extending from 9:51 to 18:14; (2) the sections peculiar to Luke contained in 3:7—8:3. These latter sections do not appear consecutively, being broken by Markan material, but they are, nevertheless, rather clearly defined.

It may be urged as an objection to the following treatment that it goes on its own way with a degree of complacency and does not take into consideration the work that has been done by others and the conclusions which they have reached. It is quite true that there is an

[1] Cf. *Cambridge Biblical Essays*, pp. 292–94.

apparent ignoring of much that has been said on the Synoptic Gospels, but this is not in any way due to a lack of appreciation of the excellence of the work done or of the very great value of its results. It has been thought advisable to avoid the literary question as far as possible as tending, on the one hand, to obscure the historical argument, and, on the other hand, to increase the length of this essay beyond its proper limits. It is not for a moment denied that the literary aspect of the problem has most important bearings on the matter; the desire has been to present the other phase. As to any failure to consider work done from the historical point of view, this is due to the fact that almost all of it, if not all, has a different approach, and thus it has been deemed wise to follow the main thread of the thought without deviating to discuss other conclusions. The wisdom, or the reverse, of this proceeding must be left to the individual judgment. In a very few cases exception has been made and an opposing position considered. To have discussed or even to have noticed the various matters of this kind would have unduly beclouded what the writer intended should be his chief interest.

A further objection may be that there is underlying the argument of this essay an assumption that a very important, if not a determining, reason for the preservation and promulgation of traditions concerning Jesus is the ability to serve a situation obtaining after his departure. This assumption, it may be charged, is seriously challenged by the fact that the gospel-writers, working at a later date, used material which *ex hypothesi* took form to meet an earlier condition. The reply to such a charge will be along several lines: the persistence in the early church of situations generally similar to those which the formulation was first designed to meet, the greater freedom of adjustment and selective power in the period when the tradition was oral and first applied to the problems of the community, the increasing disinclination to interfere with apostolic tradition, and the fact that in some cases alterations due to needs existent at the time of the writing of the gospels can be detected. Moreover, is there not underlying such a criticism an assumption that there was a pre-resurrection tradition of more or less fixity? Is it not nearer the fact to say that the literature is a product of the movement and bears the marks of the problems amid which it arose and for the solution of which it was designed?

I. AN EXAMINATION OF THE MATERIAL CONTAINED IN LUKE 9:51—18:14

We shall first pass in review that mass of material which is found in Luke 9:51—18:14, and which is known by various designations, such as "The Great Interpolation," "The Perean Section," etc. In this material the points of contact with Mark are reduced to a minimum and the peculiarly Lukan material is predominant. As already stated, the purpose of examining this material is to discover the interests of the early church which were served by it and to determine as accurately as possible their time and place.

1. THE GENERAL MISSIONARY INTEREST

It does not require a very close study of the section before us to show that one of the interests served by it is the general missionary activity of the Christian community. The statement of the appointment of the Seventy, the instructions given to them, the classes among which they labored are in close alignment with it.[1] It will be observed that the function of these messengers is purely a missionary one. There is no word of their selection for instruction by Jesus as there is of the Twelve. They are appointed to give a specific message and to do a specific work (vs. 9). The first matter that impresses one in reading this account is the number—seventy. It appears nowhere else in connection with the work of Jesus, and it is rather surprising to find that such a number of competent evangelists were available. The number seventy, which varies with seventy-two, is a natural number, and, at the same time, a somewhat artificial one. When the expanding interests of the church called for assistants to the Twelve, we find the seven deacons, the seventy (seventy-two) evangelists. In the predilection of the Jews for such numbers is found one reason for the choice, while the analogy of the seventy (seventy-two) elders who counseled with Moses might be adduced as another. The number suggests a time when the evangelizing task of the church had become too great for the Twelve. The emphasis placed upon the house in this tour of the Seventy suggests the important part played by the house in primitive Christianity.[2]

[1] Luke 10:1-24.

[2] Cf. Acts 2:46; 5:42; 8:3; 9:32 ff.; chap. 10; 12:12; Col. 4:15; Philem., chap. 2.

The impression regarding Jesus is that very much of his work was done in connection with the synagogues and in the open air. Assuredly some of his activity was in houses, just as some of the early Christian activity was in synagogues, but the emphasis on the house is suggestive. A rather striking phrase meets us in this account—"son of peace." In early Christian thought peace was one of the possessions of the true Christian. Χάρις καὶ εἰρήνη is a frequent combination. Is a "son of peace" a Christian, and is the evangelist to search out the house of such a one as a place from which to work? These verses are quite intelligible from the standpoint of a statement of regulations of primitive Christian evangelists. A Christian house is to be the base of operations and the prohibition of the long Jewish salutations is to prevent secondary matters from interfering with that which is of supreme importance. The injunction to "eat such things as are set before you" looks in the direction of a relaxation of the customs regarding clean and unclean. It points to a time when the work of Christian evangelists brought them into intimate contact with others than rigid Jews. Was this the case in the ministry of Jesus? The command to wipe off the dust from their feet against a rejecting city is very Jewish, but indicates that the activity of these men extended to others than orthodox Jews. The Jew is said to have shaken off the dust of Samaria when he left its unclean soil. The verses containing the woes on the cities have a twofold tendency. There is a distinctly favorable inclination to the extra-Palestinian cities represented by Tyre and Sidon, while the woes pronounced on the Jewish cities seem to indicate a rejection of the Christian message by the Jews and to reflect a time when the Christians would be interested in recalling any word of Jesus which represented the anger of God as falling on the Jews for such rejection.

The verses 17–24 reflect a stage when the missionary work of the church has met with some success and some failure. The exorcism of demons—the spectacular part of the work of the church—has made the greater impression and threatens to engross the attention of the Christians to the exclusion of the moral and spiritual aspects of their task.[1] This is very primitive and points to a time when the gifts of the Spirit were still a unique possession. The partial failure is shown in vss. 21 ff. The message of the preacher has not met with approval and acceptance on the part of the influential classes, but it is in the main, if not exclusively, by the lower and humble people that its appeal has been answered. The word of Jesus that it was the will of the Father

[1] Vss. 17–19.

that "babes" should receive the revelation would be of immense value in such a situation. The statement of Paul to the Corinthians[1] might be considered here.

These indications tend to show that this tradition serves interests which would emerge when the church began systematically to expand the scope of her activities. This expansion necessitated the use of a larger number of evangelists than the Twelve, instructions for missionaries in their new work, and explanations of the phenomena attendant upon their work.

The parable of the Supper contained in 14:15–24 manifests the missionary interest in a most striking manner. There can be little doubt that the supper which is prepared represents the kingdom with its blessing. The invitation has been extended to those with whom the host had more or less intimate relations, people who might be expected to appreciate the honor and eagerly to embrace the opportunity. Their astounding conduct could not fail to arouse the ire of the despised and rejected benefactor. He in turn meets the situation with conduct equally strange, in that he sends his servants to gather from the most unlikely places—the lanes and streets—people who had hitherto seemed to be at the farthest remove from those who were originally invited to enjoy the hospitality and generosity of the lord of the supper. Still more striking is the command to furnish his table with guests even to the extent of constraint. The keen disappointment and righteous indignation of the master is revealed by the stern statement that the refusal of his invitation brings absolute exclusion from the joys of the feast.

The most probable interpretation of this parable is that it sets forth the rejection of the gospel of the kingdom and its blessings by the Jews and their acceptance by the Gentiles. The situation reflected would be that of the early church in those days when she was feeling the obligation to press beyond the limits which had hitherto circumscribed her endeavors, and to give the message of redemption to people whom she had hitherto not considered eligible and who had been looked upon as having no claim on the blessings of the kingdom. The forces which brought about such a feeling of obligation are not to be discussed here, but the very essence of the gospel on its religio-ethical side was universalism. It is very evident that part of the early narrow, restricted community of Jewish Christians did break the "insidious bar" and "follow the gleam." But the very existence of the parable in its present

[1] I Cor. 1:26 ff.

form shows that this step was not taken without serious questioning as to its propriety. There was a question of tremendous import to be answered: How could it be that the heritage of the chosen people was to be taken away and given to those "without the pale"? In the time of Paul this question was insistent and the mighty mind of the apostle grappled with it. His solution is contained in the letter to the Romans, chaps. 9–11. How important a question it was and how bitterly contested is seen with some clearness in the situations discussed in Acts, chaps. 10, 11, 15, and in the long struggle between Paul and the Judaizers. This parable explains the matter by two implicit statements: (1) Those to whom the invitation was first extended, namely, the Jews, had wantonly refused it. (2) By a direct command of the master of the feast the invitation is given to those without.

The situation thus reflected is that of the early days of missionary activity, when the barriers which had kept the church's endeavor entirely within the Jewish nation were being broken down and the gospel was being carried to the Gentiles. How great an advance and how perplexing a question this was we shall not comprehend unless we succeed in appreciating, in a measure, the strong and deep Jewish convictions of the early Palestinian Christians, especially those of Jerusalem. The foundations of their universe were being removed and it was inevitable that intense and bitter opposition should arise. If in this situation the missionary leaders, men with keener insight and broader horizons than their fellows, could adduce a tradition that Jesus had taught them that this would be the line of development—if the missionary endeavor of the church could be reinforced by an *ipse dixit* of the Master—it would be of immense value and importance. Such a tradition we have in the verses under discussion.

The inimitable parables of the fifteenth chapter come under this general missionary interest. The introductory verses to the parables which show how Jesus associated intimately with publicans and sinners, and which contain the Pharisaic protest against this intimacy, can easily be understood as rendering service in such a situation as that in which Peter is described as finding himself in Acts 10:10; 11:3 ff. If the Master had eaten with sinners the disciple is not above him. This would furnish a most powerful argument in favor of the broader and more generous spirit which was reaching out with the gospel to those beyond. The parables themselves, so well known, bear directly on missionary endeavor. The ratio of ninety-nine to one is not of national significance; to consider it as such would be to make a mere incident of the parable the important matter. The parables of the Lost Sheep and Coin are not polemics against the Jews nor arguments for the Gentile mission as such. They are rather arguments, the more potent because so apposite, setting forth the urgency of saving the lost, and the "imperative" of missionary activity. If there is significance in the ratio of the numbers, it is to show the value of such work, even if it appears insignificant in results. It is the qualitative rather than the quantitative emphasis.

The third parable, that of the Prodigal Son, has a similar point if we go no farther than the twenty-fourth verse. The point is made in a somewhat different manner, but it is the same thought that is emphasized, namely, the supreme necessity and value of the work of saving the lost. The joy of the father and the glad willingness of the reception of the wayward one reproduced in the attitude of the missionaries and Christians generally would be of no little value in their work. If the Father so receives the repentant sinner, surely his followers must not refuse. The incident of the elder brother appears to have another interest. Does it reflect the opposition to missionary endeavor which was much in evidence in the early Christian community according to our sources ? The visit of Peter to Caesarea was followed by a summons to explain his attitude and conduct.[1] It might well be that the story of the elder brother was an answer to this hostility to the broader sphere of activity and the more generous spirit which was manifesting itself in the missionary wing of the church.

So much for the interest of the church's general missionary activity. The questions now confront us: At what place and at what time did such situations obtain as seem to be reflected in the sections which have just been discussed ? There are three phases of the church's missionary endeavor set forth: (1) In the sending of the Seventy with the accompanying instructions there is little, if anything, to show the area to which their labors were to be confined. It is doubtless a Palestinian mission— the whole atmosphere is Jewish—but whether it is a mission which includes Gentiles or is limited to Jews is not easy to determine. We are, however, safe in saying that it represents a missionary activity in a territory beyond that which the Twelve were able to comprehend. The questions as to the authority of those who were not of the Twelve and the conduct of missionaries were such as must early have created no little difficulty. In what place would a pronouncement on such questions be made ? Undoubtedly in Jerusalem. Jerusalem was not only the headquarters for Christian activity, it was also the seat of the

[1] Acts 11:1 ff.

Twelve with whatever authority accrued to them. Such a position of leadership and prominence is shown in Acts 4:32–35; 6:1 ff.; 8:14. Moreover, we are told that the apostles remained there after the persecution had scattered the members of the Jerusalem communities abroad throughout the land.[1] That it would be from their circle or from their community that such a pronouncement on this new activity would issue is favored by several things: (1) The apostles were the channels of tradition and from them must come the words of Jesus. (2) The position of the Jerusalem church with its apostolic leaders in the council of Acts, chap. 15.[2] The position of James in that church is to be explained on the ground of his relationship to Jesus. That Jerusalem was and remained the center of Christian activity for a considerable time—that she was the mother-church to which all others looked with a certain esteem and deference—is witnessed by the attitude of Paul in the controversy just referred to and by his earnest desire to win the favor of the Jerusalem church, as shown by his conciliatory efforts in gathering contributions and his endeavor to avoid occasions of offense.[3] (3) There was no other center which was of sufficient importance or enjoyed sufficient prestige to enable it to speak at such a time.

As to the time at which such a situation obtained, we are dependent on the account in the Acts.[4] With the exception of the Pentecostal

[1] Acts 8:1.   [2] Cf. also Gal., chaps. 1, 2.

[3] E.g., the assumption of a vow, Acts 21:23 ff.

[4] A criticism might issue against some of the arguments advanced in this discussion to the effect that too much reliance is placed on the Acts of the Apostles and too large an assumption made of its historical accuracy. Such a point would not seem to the writer to be well taken. It is but a general accuracy that is assumed. The arguments rest, not on details in Acts, but on movements and tendencies which seem to bear the marks of verisimilitude and which in some cases have corroborative testimony. For example, there may be reason for questioning some of the details of the imprisonment of the apostles as recorded in Acts 5:17 ff., but that by no means necessarily invalidates the general statement of imprisonment and that at the hands of the officials to whom it is ascribed. Similarly, some features of the Samaritan mission may fail to carry conviction of accuracy without involving a refusal to accept the general fact of missionary expansion to Samaria. In general outline we must depend upon Acts for our knowledge of the lines along which Christianity moved in its onward march, and the statements of the book regarding the large features of development and expansion seem worthy of credence.

The criticism might carry farther to the point of objecting to what might appear to be a very different attitude toward the two books generally admitted to proceed from the same author. It may be said that the historicity of the Acts of the Apostles is assumed while that of the Third Gospel is tacitly challenged. The first point has just been considered. Already it has been pointed out (p. 13) that this essay does

outburst (and that is really not an exception) the activity of the early Christians as set forth in chaps. 1–7 of this book was confined entirely to Jerusalem. It is, of course, more than probable that isolated Christians and perhaps isolated communities of Christians existed outside Jerusalem at this period. There was such a group at Damascus very soon after the dispersion of Christians from Jerusalem (Acts 9:1 ff.). But so far as our sources take us, there was no definite or widespread propaganda outside Jerusalem until after the death of Stephen. At that time the church which was at Jerusalem suffered persecution and "they were all scattered abroad throughout the regions of Judea and Samaria, except the apostles. . . . . They therefore that were scattered abroad went everywhere preaching the word." There seems to be no good reason for doubting the general accuracy of this statement. We know that the church did break beyond the Jerusalem limits and such an incident as that described has the marks of verisimilitude. When the young organization embarked on such a project as this there would be insistent need of an authoritative basis for such work to encourage missionaries and to silence objections, as well as to give directions which should govern the new enterprise. In such a situation emphasis upon the tradition of the mission of the Seventy would be natural.

Passing to the second phase, that represented in the parable of the Supper, we have the missionary situation after the appeal has been made to the Jews and has met with but a scant measure of success. One of the interesting phenomena of the development and spread of early Christianity is the comparative silence regarding its progress in Palestine apart from Jerusalem. Were the bonds of Judaism too strong to be broken, the patriotic desire for a world-ruling kingdom too deeply rooted to be removed? But the early Christian missionaries were Jews and to them the refusal of the gospel by their compatriots and its acceptance by others constituted a problem of the most serious kind. Amid such questionings the parable of the Supper would serve as a solution and would perform a function beyond that which it could exercise in any other situation we know. Again, we see that the probable place of issue is Jerusalem, and the time would be the early part of the Gentile

not concern itself with the question of historicity, but is engaged in another task. Regarding such a tacit challenging the following is evident upon even slight reflection: The fact that certain traditions owe their preservation and literary formulation to the necessity of meeting needs in the early Christian community in no way necessarily impairs the essential historicity of these traditions. The presence or extent of modification induced by the exigencies of the time when they received oral or written form is another problem.

mission. That is to say, it comes from the period when the Palestinian Christians were gradually reaching out with the gospel to those who were not their fellow-countrymen before the Gentile activity of Paul and the Antioch church.[1]

The third phase, the fifteenth chapter, comes from a situation very similar to that just outlined, namely, when the question of contact with those who were unclean from a Jewish point of view was before the community and when the value and importance of mission work required elucidation and emphasis. As in the case of the previous sections, the place where this question would become acute was Jerusalem and the time would be at the dawn of the church's wider mission.

Thus we have these three sections, strongly missionary in character, falling in tolerably well with situations and needs which we know to have existed in the Jewish-Christian community at Jerusalem in the very early years of its life. It is, of course, impossible to fix accurately the date, but the period 35 A.D.–50 A.D. would meet the facts fairly well. The year 35 A.D. is an approximate date for the commencement of missionary endeavor, and by 50 A.D. the emphasis was being shifted from the general question as to the propriety of a Gentile propaganda to the narrower question of the admission of Gentiles to Christian status and privileges apart from the observance of certain Jewish requirements. As to the formulation of such traditions at this time as against their previous existence and emphasis one cannot but wonder at the tardiness of the apostles in moving out to larger spheres if they possessed the definite declarations regarding mission work which now appear in our gospels. Moreover, if the universalism of some of the traditions was

[1] Cf. Acts 8:26 ff.; chap. 10; 11:19–26. It may be urged that the parable of the Supper would function as well after the Gentile mission of Paul as in the first break of the Christians with the Jews and the corresponding turning of the Gentiles. That is to say, the Jewish Christians always intended to go to the Gentiles with the gospel, but not in Paul's way, and this is a reflection of that later phase of the perplexing problem. Against this may be placed the real inner struggle of the Jerusalem Christians when the first overtures to the Gentiles were made by Peter and others. It is highly probable that a tradition such as this would rise in the keenness of the initial contest. Secondly, there was little remaining of the Gentile question after Paul had done his work. His success was too overwhelming. Whatever was the actual result of the Jerusalem conference, the intensity of the problem of a Gentile mission could never be the same afterward. Moreover, the general Jerusalemic character of the material in this whole section tells against the later formulation of this paragraph. The center of missionary activity and missionary struggle was transferred from Jerusalem to Greek soil after the apostles left that city, and this greatly decreases the probability of such a tradition arising in this latter environment.

existent, one cannot fail to be amazed at the difficulties which Paul and others had to overcome in practicing it. Is it not at least probable, in view of the historical fact of the confinement of apostolic and Christian work to Jerusalem for a number of years, that it was the essence of the movement itself combined with the external situation which drove Christianity out to a wider conquest? In such a case it is quite comprehensible that these traditions were given form in the place and at the time when the need for them was most acute.

II. THE SAMARITAN INTEREST

There is another interest found in the material under consideration which might have been subsumed under the previous section, but it is of such a definite character and of such importance that a separate treatment has been thought proper. It is what we may call the Samaritan interest. Nowhere else in the Synoptics do the Samaritans come into prominence as in this peculiarly Lukan material. In fact, Samaria or the Samaritans are mentioned but once in the Synoptics outside the section Luke 9:51—18:14. This is in Matt. 10:5, where an injunction is given to the twelve disciples to avoid any Samaritan city. In the Fourth Gospel two rather curious references to the Samaritans appear. The fourth chapter is for the most part concerned with the conversation of Jesus and the Samaritan woman. A very striking parenthesis occurs in vs. 9: "For the Jews have no dealings with the Samaritans." In a passage still more striking[1] the Jews are represented as saying to Jesus: "Say we not well that thou art a Samaritan and hast a demon?" In this Lukan material, however, the Samaritans occupy a position which, while not large absolutely, is of great importance by reason of contrast and by reason of the striking character of the passages containing the allusions. These passages are: (1) 9:51–56, in which the unwillingness of the Samaritans of a certain village to receive Jesus and extend him hospitality calls forth from the "Boanerges," on the one hand, a desire for vengeance, and from Jesus, on the other hand, a mild rebuke of his disciples' impetuosity; (2) the parable of the Good Samaritan, 10:25 ff.; and (3) the story of the healing of the ten lepers, only one of whom, a Samaritan, returned to express gratitude for the benefits received, 17:11 ff. That these people, so thoroughly neglected elsewhere in the Synoptics, should occupy such a position of prominence in these nine chapters surely merits our attention. The probable significance of the phenomenon we shall discuss later.

[1] John 8:48.

We must turn aside for a moment to consider the relationship and feelings which existed between the orthodox Jews and the Samaritans. There is little reason to doubt the essential historicity of the story of the origin of the Samaritan people as given in II Kings 17:3 ff., although it is probable that more than one Assyrian king, possibly three, figured in the importations of colonists. The population resulting from the deportation of the inhabitants of the Northern Kingdom and the introduction of foreigners from various conquered countries to take their places was known by the name of Samaritan. However strong a strain of Israelitish blood was retained by the resulting mixed race, it was inevitable that the Jews who prided themselves on the maintenance of purity of blood should despise and look with contempt on those who persisted in calling themselves בְּנֵי יִשְׂרָאֵל without possessing the right so to do. This contempt is shown by the rabbinical term for this people, כּוּתִים.[1]

The exclusive policy of the rigid Jews would compel them to refuse recognition to a people of mixed blood, whose religion was under grave suspicion of containing foreign elements.[2] The old cleavage between North and South would easily revive to deepen the difference, and the politico-religious barrier thus formed would be hard to surmount. How formidable this barrier was is seen in the building of the temple on Mount Gerizim, to which the Samaritans could have been driven only after being convinced that reconciliation was impossible. The most frequent references to the relations which existed between the Jews and the Samaritans are found in Josephus, and while one does not receive the statements without caution, there is little reason to doubt that he represents the general attitude with fair accuracy. In the interbiblical literature there are two references to the Samaritan people which indicate the hostility and contempt which a rigid Jew felt toward them. The first is in the Wisdom of Ben Sirach:[3] "With two nations is my soul vexed and the third is no nation: They that sit upon the mountain of Seir, and the Philistines, and the foolish people that dwelleth in Shechem." In the Testaments of the Twelve Patriarchs (Levi, chap. 7) we have the statement: "From this day shall Shechem be called the city of fools." The testimony of the rabbinical literature is not uniform, but there are not lacking indications that with many of the Jews the hostility was an abiding one. In some of its Samaritan

[1] Cf. Cuthah, II Kings 17:24.
[2] Cf. II Kings 17:33 ff.
[3] 50:25 ff.

passages the New Testament gives an interesting light on the matter. The statement of Matthew,[1] in which Jesus is represented as forbidding the missionary apostles to go into any city of the Samaritans, but to "go rather to the lost sheep of the house of Israel," sets forth strongly the difference which was made between the two peoples.   The fact that such a word was allowed to remain in the mouth of Jesus at the time of the composition of Matthew is extremely suggestive in this regard. The refusal of the Samaritans to receive Jesus and his followers, as shown in Luke,[2] manifests the same attitude.   The Johannine references in the fourth chapter, where the woman practically refuses a draught of water to Jesus on the ground that she is a Samaritan while he is a Jew, followed by the explanatory parenthesis mentioned above, "For the Jews have no dealings with [ask no favors of(?)] the Samaritans," show that the distrust and dislike were deep and strong.   The last reference in the gospels is that in which the term is applied to Jesus himself, and expresses the strongest contempt and antipathy.[3]   These statements in the gospels can be explained on no other ground than the existence of an intensely bitter feeling between those who considered themselves of pure Jewish blood and faith and the inhabitants of the central district of Palestine.[4]

In the outline of the spread and development of early Christianity as presented in the Acts of the Apostles we find that no Christian work was done among the Samaritans before the dispersion which followed upon the persecution of the Jerusalem church.   This is the case in spite of the stated command of the risen Lord to be witnesses in Judea and Samaria, and so forth.[5]   In fact, when such work was undertaken it was in a way as great an innovation as the Gentile mission.   The easy way in which the spread of the gospel among the Samaritans is recorded in the eighth chapter of Acts gives no hint of the difficulties, internal and external, which beset the Samaritan mission.   Apparently it was a triumphant conquest on the part of Philip and the apostles Peter and John.   Practically nothing is known of the Samaritan Christians in any organized way and it is probable that the terrible experiences of 67 A.D.–70 A.D. shattered any such work.   But that the Samaritan people as such were not evangelized is to be inferred from the massacre

[1] 10:5.   [2] 9:51 ff.   [3] John 8:48.

[4] As to the persistence of feeling between Jews and Samaritans, see Schürer, *Geschichte des jüdischen Volkes*, 4. Aufl., II, 18–23; *The Jewish People in the Time of Jesus Christ*, Div. II, Vol. I, pp. 5–8.

[5] Acts 1:8.

of the Galileans under the procuratorship of Cumanus, 48–52 A.D.[1] The references in the gospels show that with the Christians the antipathy persisted, which would be very doubtful if such a sweeping Christianizing had taken place.

It would seem to be inevitable that, when the Christian missionaries went on Samaritan soil with the gospel message and offered the blessings of the kingdom to the people toward whom the orthodox Jews entertained such feelings, such a procedure would meet with strong opposition. A study of the early chapters of Acts shows clearly that the Christians at Jerusalem did not for some time differentiate themselves from the orthodox Jews save on the question of the messiahship of Jesus.[2] The whole of the controversy over circumcision ultimately rests on this fact. This being so, it must have seemed to strict Jews, in spite of points of contact between Jews and Samaritans, a casting of the children's bread to dogs to give the promises to the schismatics of the middle country. The name of the Samaritan missionary—Philip— and his appointment among the Seven raises the interesting question whether or not he was a Hellenist and possibly of more liberal views than many of the Palestinian Jews.

Bearing in mind these two facts, (1) the steady and persistent dislike which obtained between Jews and Samaritans and which Christianity did not easily obliterate from the Jewish heart, (2) that nowhere in the New Testament apart from the eighth chapter of Acts (this is shadowed by the Simon Magus story) are the Samaritans mentioned with approval except in this peculiarly Lukan section, we proceed to discover what interest could prompt or be served by such a departure from the otherwise constant attitude. It would, of course, be easy to say that it was the universalism of Jesus manifesting itself. But there are grave difficulties in the way of such a solution.

The allusions themselves are instructive. The first one[3] recognizes the general attitude of the Samaritans toward the Jews and, conversely, that of the Jews toward the Samaritans. The occasion of the hostility is said to be the purpose of Jesus to go to Jerusalem. Undoubtedly the apostles thought they were showing true loyalty to their Master and true devotion to their nation in their request for vengeance, and the rebuke of Jesus in favor of the despised enemies must have sounded strange in their ears. Yet it is a very mild form of approval, if that be the correct term, which the passage shows. The parable of the Good

[1] Josephus, *Ant.*, XX, 118–36; *B.J.*, II, 232–46.

[2] Acts 3:1 ff., chap. 13; 5:12(?), 30.   [3] Luke 9:51–56.

Samaritan sets this people in a much better light. The story and its
setting are too well known to require repetition. It will not be disputed
that the central teaching of the story is that of neighborliness, but that
does not entirely explain the selection of the Samaritan as its shining
example. It is true that the Samaritan had the advantage of proximity
in being chosen for such a purpose, but the point could have been made
equally well, if not better, had a Gentile been pressed into service. It
is not easy to think that the three classes of men mentioned—priest,
Levite, and Samaritan—merely chanced to be selected to illustrate the
point. There is a suspicion that there is underlying a plea for the
people whose representative could rise higher in the scale of mercy and
generous service than the religious leaders of the self-complacent Jews.
The Samaritan appears here in strong contrast with those who were
supposed to typify the best in Israel's life, and the inference is inevitable
that such a people could not be wholly bad. The third instance is also
a case in which the Samaritan is set in the best possible light by contrast.
Of the ten who had been the recipients of the blessing of healing only
one cared to return to thank his benefactor. Here the Samaritan is
not the model of service and neighborliness as above, but he stands forth
as an example of gratitude. The marked contrast with the others,
ostensibly Jews, is expressed in the words, "Were there none found that
returned to give glory to God, save this stranger?" The three allusions
seem to be in climactic order of favorableness, but it would not be well
to press such a point. It is difficult to avoid the conclusion that we have
here traditions formulated or emphasized to meet the same general
situation. Can we discover a situation which would be met by
them?

The previous discussion makes it evident that it was the inception
and process of the Samaritan mission. The very fact that Jews brought
the new message could not fail to arouse antagonism among the Samaritans. To them the new propaganda would be little more than an
attempt to induce them to acknowledge the purity and superiority of
the rigid Jews. It does not require a great stretch of the imagination
to conceive that some villages showed decided opposition to the missionaries, thus discouraging them and arousing the slumbering fires
of hatred. In such a case what more powerful argument could be used
than the story of the Samaritan churlishness, the refusal of Jesus to
execute vengeance, and the calm turning from one village to another?
It is an inimitable piece of work, looked at from the standpoint of what
might easily be the pressing needs of the Samaritan mission.

But all the hostility did not emanate from Samaria. The Jerusalem Christians, some of them at least, were far too strict Jews to look on this proffer of the kingdom to these semi-aliens with equanimity. Very easily could mutterings against the movement arise, and even positive criticism. With what tremendous force could a word of the Master be used, if one could be obtained, in such a situation! Here we have the Good Samaritan, with the positive qualities of ethical righteousness, towering above the religious representatives of the Jews. If a Samaritan could be of this sort, surely the people were worthy of the best evangelizing efforts of the Christians. The great commandment is love to God and man. Up to the point of missionary departure it does not appear that the church had placed any broad emphasis on the latter. As soon as it began to be understood, the wider appeal was inevitable. The Samaritan is your neighbor; therefore see to it that he gets the same opportunity for blessing as you.[1] This story would be of real value in combating what would seem to be an unavoidable opposition to a Samaritan mission. A similar use could be made of the healing of the ten lepers. That the only one of the ten Palestinians who returned to acknowledge the benefits received was a Samaritan, a stranger, would tend to show that these people were not wanting in proper feelings of gratitude and would acknowledge their indebtedness to their benefactors beyond many who plumed themselves on their pure Jewish extraction. The manifestation of thankfulness would do much to break down the bars of prejudice.

Two lines of argument, then, seem to suggest that these Samaritan sections gained prominence at the time of the dispersion of the Jerusalem Christians, mentioned in Acts 8:1-2. These lines are: (1) the very high degree of probability that such a mission would create antagonism and opposition on the part of Jews who could not quite forget the deep cleft between them and their neighbors; (2) the isolated character of these phenomena of favorable consideration of the Samaritans in the whole field of primitive Christian literature. It scarcely needs argument to show that the place where such traditions would be of use, and, therefore, assume the form in which they could be used, was Jerusalem. There the apostles remained even in the days of the persecution (an indication of the closeness with which they adhered to Judaism); to them and to the church in that place the rebuffed missionaries would naturally turn for encouragement and instruction. There also would

---

[1] It will be noticed that there is a change of application of the term "neighbor." The Samaritan is the neighbor in vs. 36, but it should be the victim of the thieves.

most naturally arise the opposition to the movement which threatened to break down the barriers which the brooding and hatred of ages had raised. Thus we find the traditions of this specific Samaritan interest aligning themselves with those of the more general missionary interest in their pragmatic character and in that Jerusalem was the place of their promulgation.

III. THE RECIPROCAL OPPOSITION OF PHARISEES AND CHRISTIANS

Readers of the gospels are so familiar with the differences which arose between Jesus and the religious leaders of his people that but scant attention is paid to features of the tradition which fit but strangely into the career of Jesus as we know it. It is not to be doubted that there was opposition between Jesus and the scribes and Pharisees, and that it was an important, in some respects a determining, factor in his career. But it may well be questioned whether the portrayal of these classes, as we have it, is quite a fair and unprejudiced one. Religious prejudice is an adept at giving a twist to the facts. Modern Jewish apologists have risen to protest against this depicting of their compatriots, and to declare the inaccuracy and inadequacy of the description.[1] From un-prejudiced Jewish sources we gain the impression that these apologists have many things in their favor.

One cannot avoid questioning whether if this hostility of the Pharisees to Jesus had ceased at his death and resurrection the bitter-ness and vituperation which some parts of our gospel story manifest would have been remembered and recorded. It does not make pleasant reading, and it is hard to believe that the early Christians would have preserved such traditions and have given them prominence if the antagonisms of the Jewish religionists to the thought and attitude of Jesus had not been transferred to his followers.

We learn from the early chapters of the Acts of the Apostles that such opposition did persist, and that it rose at last into persecution. It is true that the Sadducees seem to have the prominent part in any proceedings against the Christians, but this may be accounted for in several ways. (1) The high priests, who possessed great authority, belonged to the Sadducean party. To them would be the most telling

---

[1] Cf. the discussion among Schürer, Abraham, Montefiore, and Menzies, in *Geschichte des jüdischen Volkes*, 4. Aufl., II, 537–79; *The Jewish People in the Time of Jesus Christ*, Div. II, Vol. II, pp. 90–125, *Jewish Quarterly Review*, XI, 626–42; *Hibbert Journal*, I, 335–46, 789–92; cf. also *Revue des études juives*, LI, 191–216; LII, 1–23.

appeal in the matter of safeguarding the national religion from everything that had in it the possibilities of inconvenience for the official class. Already in the case of the death of Jesus the Pharisees, generally their bitter opponents, had joined hands with them. It was an easy matter to continue the alliance against the followers of Jesus. (2) The Sadducees were dominant in influence in the Sanhedrin, and were the officials. To act legally in a matter of this sort their interest and support must be enlisted. (3) The doctrine of the resurrection which the Christians preached would be offensive to them.

But the jealous party in the matter of opposing innovations on the national religion was the Pharisees. This had been true at all times since the Maccabean period. The interference of the authorities with the apostles in which the Sadducees appear to be the leaders[1] was but a herald of the coming storm. Even in these cases the Pharisees would not lack representatives in the punitive court—the Sanhedrin. It is quite possible that they were the real instigators of the opposition, as in the case of Jesus. At any rate, when severe persecution makes its appearance at the time of the death of Stephen and during the following months it is not a Sadducee, but a Pharisee of the Pharisees, that is the moving spirit and the most active agent. Here again the authority of the high priest has to be invoked to give an air of legality to the matter.[2] The incentive to move against Stephen and the sect of which he was a member is very similar to that which actuated the Pharisees in their opposition to Jesus. The sanctity of their religion was being invaded, its permanency and authority disputed. There are many indications that the Pharisees were the moving spirits in the persecution of the early church, working, of course, in conjunction with the priestly authorities, who would be aroused on personal rather than on religious grounds.

What situation do the sections of Luke under consideration reflect? The first section is one of considerable length and extends from 11:37 to 12:12. It is readily admitted that much of this fits well in the ostensible situation and represents a fairly acute stage of the controversy between Jesus and the Pharisees. But there are features which suggest a later situation. The intensely Jewish atmosphere of this section is shown in 11:41, "But give for alms those things which are within and behold all things are clean unto you." That is to say, that which makes

[1] Acts 4:1 ff.; 5:17.

[2] Acts 9:1. As to Paul's energy and persistence in persecution, cf. Gal. 1:13, 23; Phil. 3:6.

clean is almsgiving.   It was among the Jews that almsgiving was almost
tantamount to righteousness.[1]   One wonders if the ἁρπαγῆς of 11:39
is material and refers to the wealth of the Pharisees when compared
with the poverty of the Christians.   It would not be hard to find there
an added cause of censure.[2]   "Ye build the tombs of the prophets and
your fathers killed them.   So ye are witnesses and consent unto the
works of your fathers: for they killed them, and ye build their tombs.
Therefore also said the wisdom of God, I will send unto them prophets
and apostles, and some of them they shall kill and persecute; that the
blood of all the prophets which was shed from the foundation of the
world may be required from this generation. . . . . Woe unto you
lawyers! for ye took away the key of knowledge: ye entered not in
yourselves and them that were entering ye hindered."   How could
it be said that these Pharisees were witnesses and participants of the
works of their fathers?   It may be that it meant that the scribes were
perpetuating the same system that killed the prophets, but that is not
an adequate explanation.   In the time of Jesus, so far as we know, no
prophet, save himself, suffered at the hands of the Pharisees.   But
the matter gains point when we link up the memory of their part in his
death, their supreme sin, with the persecution and death of Christians.[3]
The combination "prophets and apostles" is very natural as coming
from a primitive Christian community.   These were two important
orders in the early church.[4]   The prophets enjoyed a place of prominence
and esteem among early Christians and their words were considered to
have authority.   With regard to the term "apostles,"[5] it is a matter of
grave doubt whether the title was given to the Twelve in the days of
Jesus.   In Eph. 4:7 ff. "apostleship" is a gift of the ascended Christ,
that is, of the Spirit, and is placed in the same list as prophets, evangelists, and so forth.   It is probable that this title was conferred on the
intimates of Jesus to mark their peculiar qualifications as witnesses of
the resurrection.   In any case the collocation "prophets and apostles"
admirably fits the situation of the early church at Jerusalem, and the
passage suggests a time when the leaders of the church were suffering

---

[1] Cf. Tob. 4:6 ff.

[2] Note the attitude of the early Christians toward wealth.

[3] Cf. Acts, chaps. 7, 8; 12:1 ff.

[4] As to the position of Christian prophets, cf. Acts 11:27; 13:1; I Cor. 12:10,
28 f.; Revelation, and patristic references.

[5] Cf. Ernest D. Burton, "The Office of Apostle in the Early Church," *American
Journal of Theology*, XVI, 561–88.

at the hands of the Jewish authorities. For such a situation and its effect on the early church the twelfth chapter of Acts may be consulted. "This generation" is to be held responsible for the whole process[1] and the penalty imposed is the abandonment of the Jews by God and the working of the power of evil among them. The rejection by the Jews of the proffered blessings of the kingdom through Jesus is set forth in vs. 52 and the greater blame attached to the νομικοί. But Luke 12:2 ff. suggests still more strongly the Apostolic age and the situation of the early church. The comforting assurance that the thing spoken secretly should have wide publicity would be of immense importance in reviving the drooping spirits of the Jerusalem Christians when, under stress of Pharisaic opposition, they had, at least for a time, to carry on their meetings secretly. It might well be that some wondered how they were to prosecute their work when publicity was prevented.[2]

That this section represents the Christian church under Pharisaic persecution seems clear from Luke 12:4 ff. There is a worse fate than bodily death, so terrible that it should be feared: the death of the soul, which death can be brought about by apostasy and denial. It is true that the Pharisees cause fear by the exercise of their persecuting power, but it is far better to suffer at their hands than to be unfaithful to God. Moreover, this suffering on their part is no indication that God has forgotten. He has numbered the hairs of their heads and everything is under his permissive control. The passage regarding confession or denial of the Son of Man would be of inestimable value in encouraging steadfastness and checking any tendency to apostasy. That such encouragement and warning were necessary stands almost in the nature of the case. The mention of the synagogues, the rulers, and the authorities in Luke 12:11 fits the Jewish-Christian situation in Jerusalem and its mission to Jews as it fits no other. The theme of the whole paragraph[3] is Christianity under persecution by the Pharisees. The Christians are to do their task, remain faithful, endure trials under the assurance of ultimate triumph. The appositeness of this section to the situation in Palestine, especially in Jerusalem, at the time of the Pharisaic opposition seems too clear to require further argument. It seems highly probable that we have here a primitive tradition regarding the Pharisaic religion and attitude adapted and brought into use in the time of its need. There does not appear to be any real reason for the

[1] Luke 11:50–51.

[2] For such prevention, cf. Acts 4:18; 5, 28; 12:12.

[3] 12:1–12.

preservation of this tradition unless it was called forth by continued opposition on the part of the sect so severely censured.

The anti-Pharisaic interest—for the expression of which we have found adequate cause—appears again in Luke 16:14-15. The section 16:14-17 seems to be composed of two originally independent parts, at least logically such, which interrupt the main thought. Vss. 14-15 contain the application to the Pharisees of the previous statements regarding the allurements and dangers of wealth, and suggest that in the gathering of their wealth their trust of the true riches had been betrayed. A further recurrence of the feeling against the Pharisees is seen in Luke 18:9-14 in the comparison of the Pharisee and the publican in their attitude of spirit in prayer. However genuine a tradition this might be from the standpoint of Jesus, it would never be of such significance as when the Christians, drawn from humble ranks, suffering privations and hardships, wondering as all Jews did why their piety was not rewarded with prosperity, became conscious of the wealth and the power and the unrighteousness of the Pharisees and oppressed with the burden of the contrast. Did the rank and file—yes, even the apostles themselves—reach this consciousness before their actual experience with the sect in Jerusalem? That their Master with his supreme insight saw thus clearly may be indisputable, but did even the clearest-visioned of his followers attain this? It is quite probable that this story gained currency in the days when the leaders of the church were antagonizing the Pharisees and when they wished to show to their half-doubting followers that in the sight of God they were the possessors of the true riches.

IV. THE EMPHASIS ON DISCIPLESHIP

In the very nature of the case the problems of discipleship, with their almost bewildering variety, would obtrude themselves very prominently in the early years of the Christian movement. The Christian body was composed of people who had broken, or were breaking, from moorings to which they had long held fast in safety and with more or less tranquillity. Many, possibly the overwhelming majority, of these people were from the humbler walks of life, uneducated, lacking in powers of self-control, creatures of impulse to a degree, suspicious and wayward, very human. The organization to which they attached themselves was new and untried, the motives which led to the attachment almost as varied as the people were numerous. It was a period of experiment, fluidity, uncertainty, and trial. The possibilities for vagaries were many, and the need of instruction, encouragement, admonition, and control urgent. It would be strange indeed if such conditions and such need had not left their mark on the traditions of the time. In the section before us the interest of control of discipleship emerges very early. The passage Luke 9:57–61, which contains some very perplexing matters if interpreted from the standpoint of Jesus, becomes interesting and illuminating when looked at from the point of view of the early Christian community and the interest now under consideration. The language is so striking that one suspects a very insistent need for a clear and strong statement of the terms of discipleship. The glad abandon of the new convert is expressed in the words, "I will follow thee whithersoever thou goest"; and is in turn met by the ardor-dampening, "The foxes have· holes and the birds of the heaven their nests, but the Son of Man hath not where to lay his head." If there were those pressing into the new movement thoughtlessly or with hopes of any material benefit in the kingdom, such a reply must have given them pause. If there be any motive of self-aggrandizement it would be better to follow foxes, for the Son of Man has nothing material to offer. It does not require a high degree of imagination to think of such motives as actuating ones. The murmuring of the Grecian Jews regarding their widows,[1] the communistic experiment,[2] and the sordidness of Ananias[3] are straws which indicate the current.

The next statement of the passage[4] is an exceedingly strange one. "Let the dead bury their own dead, but go thou and publish the kingdom of God." On the face of it, the saying seems perfectly heartless, but it is somewhat intelligible if we can think of it as meeting a situation when the performance of filial duties threatened to interfere with a matter that seemed to be of supreme importance. It is probable that missionary tasks necessitated some hardships which might well cause some faint souls to waver. Such a word as this, as coming from the lips of Jesus and touching a thing of such importance to the Jews as decent burial,[5] would teach that true discipleship and membership in the kingdom called for the acme of self-abnegation. After this word, any plea on this or similar grounds would be ruled out of court. Very similar, but with a slightly different emphasis, is the third statement and reply.[6] One cannot but feel that the answer to a very natural desire to bid farewell to friends is harsh and unyielding. It is a minor thing for which to deem one unworthy of the kingdom. But if the statement be applied

---

[1] Acts 6:1 ff.   [3] Acts 5:1 ff.   [5] Cf. Tob. 1:18; 2:3 ff.
[2] Acts 4:32–36.   [4] Vss. 59–60.   [6] Vss. 61–62.

to a time when social and domestic ties and duties and the bond of blood
were threatening to interfere with devotion to the new movement and
its tasks, its value as coming from Jesus is instantly seen. That such
a situation arose frequently in the early church is easy to believe. The
scantiness of our sources and the unlikelihood of such a phase being
directly recorded does not permit a definite assignment to a specific
situation. The epistolary literature of the New Testament reflects
similar or analogous situations. The point is that the paragraph represents Jesus as requiring of disciples absolute devotion and sacrifice.
If Jesus demanded these or similar things no disciple who recognized
his lordship could refuse them.

The same interest is clearly seen in a passage which has been discussed under the previous topic, Luke 12:1 ff. Here the disciples are
exhorted to steadfastness and fidelity under persecution, evidently a
persecution on the part of the Pharisees. The designation of the disciples
as friends (φίλοι) in 12:4 is a fine touch and would serve to dignify
discipleship. There is a strong exhortation to fidelity and watchfulness in 12:35 ff. The "burning lamp" and "girded loins" are striking
figures of watchfulness and preparedness. This would seem to represent
a time when the Christians were beginning to wonder at the delay of the
Lord's return, which they had thought from the beginning would be
immediate. With the wonderment are mingled some disappointment
and a relaxing of vigilance, perhaps also a looseness of conduct and an
indifference to work. The promise that the Master will come suddenly
and himself minister to their needs and exalt them would fit such a
situation excellently. That such situations of impatience and wonderment did exist is shown by Acts 1:6-7; I Cor., chap. 15; I Thess.
4:13 ff. It is a Christian recurrence of the problem, part of which the
Jews solved by the doctrine of the resurrection.

There is a further appearance of the interest in Luke 12:49-53.
It is not hard to think that a religious movement such as Christianity
interfered with social and family relations. We scarcely need to look
beyond our own generation and its denominationalism for proof. Amid
the bitter differences which could so easily obtain when some members
of a family or group embraced the new faith, what more telling word
from the Master could be pressed into service than this? One of the
purposes of the Lord's life on earth was that these divisions and struggles
might come to pass. The pragmatic value of the passage is very evident.

Another outcropping of the interest in discipleship occurs in Luke
14:25 ff. The demands made on the true and worthy disciple and the

characteristics of such a one are here set forth. The previous paragraph has suggested how bitter an opposition could arise when Christianity differentiated itself from Judaism and began to be recognized as a different sect. The bitterness of feeling, the depth of resentment, and the measures of persecution which could obtain among members of the same household have a modern analogy on many mission fields. It would not be at all surprising if, in the face of social opposition and the hostile forces of domestic relations exerted in the same direction, not a few converts wavered in their resolution and threatened to apostasize. In such a case the reference to hatred of those nearest by ties of blood and to the bearing of severe discipline as typified by the term "cross," the reference to these as absolute essentials to true discipleship and, therefore, to participation in the blessings of the kingdom, would be a most potent force in steadying the wavering and restraining the feet of those who were faltering. The fact of apostasy in the early Christian community needs little argument. As soon as our sources expand, we find it appearing in Paul's work and causing him no little embarrassment and sorrow. Such apostates would be the occasion of much scandal and a serious hindrance to other converts. For the purpose of preventing hasty professions of Christian faith which would later be quickly denied under stress of privation, persecution, or opposition of any kind, the illustrations regarding counting the cost and planning the whole campaign in order to avoid the mockery of one's fellows and the sting of defeat would be strong weapons. These two illustrations are followed by the categorical statement that nothing under heaven must be allowed to stand between the disciple and the claims of his Lord.[1]

These passages do not complete the number which are concerned with statements regarding discipleship. Luke 17:1-10 concerns itself ultimately with the community life. The "little ones" are believers and some persons or things are causing them to stumble. It is not possible to say with any degree of assurance what are the causes of offense, but the seriousness of the matter is indisputable. It may be that the persecutors are here referred to and that on them the curse falls. But with equal, even with greater, probability, if we take "thy brother" of vs. 3 into consideration, the reference is to the treatment of the weak brother by some stronger one. This treatment is according to a standard which tends to discourage the weaker one and cause him to fall away. The seriousness of such a situation is clear. The exhortations to forgiveness[2] breathe the spirit of some generous soul and suggest

[1] Vs. 33.   [2] Vss. 3-4.

that too stringent demands had been made by some puritanical disciplinarians and forgiveness and restoration withheld.

The following verses, especially 7–10, seem to indicate that some were beginning to plume themselves on the amount and quality of the service they were rendering. This might easily happen where the labors of some had been more successful than those of others. Thoughts would naturally fly to the greater rewards of the kingdom, and such a spirit would have large possibilities of creating discontent and dissension.[1] It would be very salutary and of great force to have a word of the Master which would tell them that after the utmost service had been rendered by them there was no cause for congratulation, but rather for humility of spirit; all they have done is but the mere fulfilment of duty. If thanks are expressed and blessing bestowed it is not on the basis of desert or merit, it is gratis.

Thus we see that the matter of discipleship bulks large in this material. There will be no inclination to deny that problems similar to those which are met by these sections arose wherever Christian communities came into being and flourished. It is simply the emergence of the human. Since this is so, it is not easy to tie down any section to a specific place or situation with any degree of assurance. But we may be confident that when these problems arose, problems which were vital to the church, no time would be lost in bringing to bear an authoritative word that would meet the situation. The place where these questions would first obtrude themselves and demand answer was almost certainly Jerusalem. The reference to the burial of the dead, the Pharisaic persecution, the impatience at the delay of the Lord's coming, and the pluming of one's self on greatness of service are primarily Jewish and Jerusalemic. While demonstration is not possible, there is much to be said in favor of the hypothesis that these traditions took form to meet situations in the Jerusalem community, or at least arose in Jerusalem, the center of apostolic tradition, to meet situations in the Christian communities on Palestinian soil.

V. THE ASCETIC INTEREST

In discussing the opposition to the Pharisees which seems to have obtained in the early church, we noticed occasional flashes of censure of their wealth-accumulating propensities combined with words of comfort to the poverty-ridden Christians. This last feature reappears

---

[1] Cf. the request of James and John and the indignation of the other disciples. Mark 10:35–41.

emphasized and strengthened in what we have called the ascetic interest. The first instance is in Luke 10:38–42 where Martha makes her appeal to Jesus against Mary. It is rather strange that the Son of Man who came "eating and drinking" should apparently rebuke the generous hospitality of his hostess. The matter takes on a new color from the standpoint of an interest which is either combating a tendency to indulgence and luxury or endeavoring to overcome the allurement of the "good things of life." The exaltation of the "good part which shall not be taken away" would serve such an interest. Whatever the interpretation of the "one thing," whether it signifies that the spiritual is to take precedence over the mere bodily necessities or refers to the simplicity of the meal, the tendency is to exalt the severe and repressive.

Again, in 11:27–28 an interest which might be called ascetic appears. The natural feelings and emotions are given a subordinate position and the spiritual is emphasized. This is the repressive element which makes religious duties override family ties and affections. The paragraph 12:13–20 sets forth an appeal to Jesus to be an arbitrator in the matter of an "inheritance." The stern refusal to deal with such matters, combined with the statement that a man's life consisteth not in the things which he possesseth, and with the parable of the Rich Fool, manifests a strong tendency against the accumulation of wealth and the indulgence which it brings and at the same time serves to exalt simplicity and sincerity of life. In agreement with this is the exhortation to avoid the chief seats at feasts and public places, with the corresponding commendation of humility, and the accompanying promise that true humility and freedom from self-seeking will gain the reward of honor and esteem, while ostentation and self-aggrandizement can meet no other end than confusion and humiliation.

It may be argued that these are tenuous threads from which to weave the fabric of an ascetic interest. It is granted that they are somewhat fragile, but not overmuch so. Is it not true that in the atmosphere of the early Christian community, with its vagueness and need of adjustment, the emphasis on asceticism could not be laid too strongly for fear of injuring an undeveloped faith? It would seem to be the part of good leadership not to urge it to the point of repulsion. The extravagant exaltation of this tendency in later times to the extent of indifference to the body and the glorification of martyrdom, as seen in the Epistles of Ignatius and the Martyrdom of Polycarp, would probably have strongly repelled the halting novices in the faith and defeated the aims of the interest.

Did a situation exist in the early church in which such an interest would play a part? We may note the experiment of that organization as recorded in Acts 2:43–45. The possession of great wealth was evidently not encouraged in the community.[1] Again, there can be little doubt that James, the brother of Jesus, early became a commanding and influential personage in the Jerusalem church.[2] His relationship to Jesus would naturally give him special claims to distinction and his dicta would have corresponding influence and weight. His Jewish strictness and rigidity on the ascetic side are shown in his attitude on the matter of clean and unclean,[3] as well as in the interference of his messengers at Antioch.[4] This, of course, proves no more than that James was a strict, unyielding Jew in these respects, but the elements which make for asceticism are there. However, in addition to this we have the statement of Hegesippus in the fifth book of his *Commentaries*, quoted by Eusebius:[5]

But James, the brother of the Lord, who, as there are many of his name, was surnamed the Just by all, from the days of our Lord until now, received the government of the church with the apostles. This apostle was consecrated from his mother's womb. He drank neither wine nor fermented liquors, and abstained from animal food. A razor never came upon his head, he never anointed with oil, and never used a bath. He alone was allowed to enter the sanctuary. He never wore woolen, but linen garments. He was in the habit of entering the temple alone, and was often found upon his bended knees, and interceding for the forgiveness of the people, so that his knees became as hard as camels' in consequence of his habitual supplication and kneeling before God.

Exception may be taken to the historicity of this passage, and probably some of the details are fanciful and apocryphal. But after due allowance has been made for legendary accretion there probably remains a residuum which indicates that James was of an ascetic temperament. It does not seem likely that such a statement arose with absolutely no foundation. This, coupled with what we know of the man from the New Testament, gives fair justification for ascribing a severe and repressive tendency to him. What is more likely than that this should appear in some of the traditions regarding Jesus and that these should be promulgated first in the Jerusalem community and made to meet any tendency to laxity and indulgence?

[1] Acts 4:32–35.

[2] Acts 15:13, 15, 22; 21:17; Gal. 1:19; 2:9, 12.

[3] Acts 15:19–20.   [4] Gal. 2:12.   [5] *H.E.*, II, 23.

VI. THE TEACHING ON EXORCISM

We pass now to one of the most difficult phases of our subject and one of no little importance. This is the teaching of this section on exorcism. Its first appearance is in connection with the return of the Seventy.[1] The Seventy are represented as rejoicing because on their missionary tour their work of preaching had been accompanied by works of exorcism, "Lord, even the demons are subject to us in thy name." The sentence can be understood only in the light of the prevailing world-view and the demonology of the time. This, however, will form a later part of our discussion. The striking thing about this passage is that, apart from a momentary flash of apparent gladness, there is no word of commendation from Jesus for this work. On the contrary, there is a very distinct rebuff to any tendency to give an important place to this species of activity. "Nevertheless, in this rejoice not that the spirits are subject to you, but rejoice that your names are written in heaven." Here the spiritual side of the work is clearly given prominence at the expense of the spectacular.

The question of exorcism crops out for a moment in Luke 13:31–33, where Jesus makes reply to the Pharisees who warn him against Herod. The reply is an oracular one and is rather colorless in respect to our discussion here. The other important place in the section where exorcism is discussed is in Luke 11:14–26. Here we seem to have two conflicting phases of the subject, the latter of which we shall discuss first. The statement regarding the man who has been delivered from an unclean spirit and who suffers the return of the demon with seven others of a more vicious type is one which has caused no little difficulty to interpreters. The only legitimate inference is that a deliverance from such a spirit is followed by a domination many times worse. Then why continue the practice? It would seem inhuman so to do. The question raises itself whether this passage does not represent a circle which is interested in showing the inferiority of exorcism as a line of religious activity and its temporary character. If this is so, it is a stronger expression of the interest manifested in the somewhat gentle rebuke of Jesus to the Seventy.

The verses which precede those which have just been discussed, namely, 11:14–23, offer some difficulty. It is the only definite case of exorcism in this whole section—in fact, in all the non-Markan material—and is on the whole unfavorable. The very fact that such activity could be connected with the name of Beelzebul shows that in some circles it

[1] Luke 10:17–20.

did not enjoy high repute. But the argument of the passage is that it is by divine power that these deeds are accomplished, and that this acquisition and exercise of power over the evil spirits is a foreshadowing of the kingdom of God, an earnest of the greater conquest to be. A stronger than "the prince of the power of the air" is working for the overthrow of evil. The implication of vs. 23 is that any opposition to this testimony is opposition to God through Jesus. It is quite possible that we have here a reply to those who denounced the practice from a circle which practiced exorcism and saw in it the promise and adumbration of the kingdom.

Have we then in these passages indications that there were two circles among early Christians which held opposing views on this subject? Let us examine whatever facts may have a bearing on the matter. In reference to the practice of exorcism by the early Christians we note that in Acts 5:16 works of healing and exorcism on the part of the apostles are said to have attracted large numbers of people from the country around Jerusalem. The opposition of the Jewish leaders seems to be closely connected with this. We have no means of determining what the "great wonders and signs" wrought by Stephen were,[1] but it is probable that casting out evil spirits had its place among them. In the Samaritan mission under the leadership of Philip we are told that his "signs" were exorcisms and that there were many of them. The story of Simon Magus gives an interesting side-light on the impression which such deeds made on a sorcerer. In Acts 8:14 ff. the power to cast out demons is dependent on the reception of the Holy Spirit, which reception was accompanied by external manifestations. On the missionary tour of Paul and Barnabas they wrought "signs and wonders" at Iconium, and unbelieving Jews stirred up opposition against them. We have also the specific case of Paul at Philippi.[2] Thus there can be no doubt that exorcism was practiced by Jewish Christians at a very early time, that it was performed under control of the Holy Spirit, and that it was exorcism in the name of Jesus.[3]

What was the Jewish attitude toward exorcism? It appears to have been more or less a custom among the Jews. This is shown by the *ad hominem* argument of Jesus in Luke 11:19, "By whom do your sons cast them out?" Unless there was a practice more or less prevalent the remark would have little point. Acts, chap. 19, is also of significance here. At Ephesus Paul came into contact with a number of itinerant exorcists of Jewish nationality. Evidently they made a profession of

[1] Acts 6:8.   [2] Acts 16:16 ff.

[3] Cf. Acts 4:30; 5:28; 16:18; Luke 10:17.

casting out demons. In the interbiblical literature the Book of Tobit presents a case in point, and it is an easy matter to trace both prophetic and legal hostility to all forms of magic.[1] The translation of Exod. 20:7 might well run, "Thou shalt not take the name of the Lord thy God for an evil purpose." The evil use of the name of Yahweh which is here forbidden cannot possibly refer to its use in swearing, because the people are frequently exhorted to swear by his name.[2] Moreover, the use of the sacred name for any such purpose as blasphemous cursing would be the last thought for a Jew. It is far more likely that the prohibition is to prevent its use in incantations and spells which conjured the evil spirit to or from its abode. Two things then are clear: (1) that the practice of sorcery was in vogue among the Jewish people, for laws are not made in advance of need and prophets do not fulminate against purely imaginary evils; (2) that there were legal prohibitions of such practices.

We must now recall that at the head of the church in Jerusalem stood a man who was a Jew of a rigid and strictly legal bent. To such a man the exorcisms which were performed would be a matter for doubt, if not a thing of abhorrence. That James had a strong following in the Jerusalem church is evidenced by the part it played later in the legalistic controversy. What is more probable than that in this circle there grew up an opposition to the practice of exorcising in the name of Jesus? To the members of this legalistic circle it was a transgression of a direct command and therefore not to be tolerated. Viewed from the standpoint of such a situation the passages on exorcism in our section become intelligible as they do on no other interpretation. Again we find our material giving indications of having emanated from the Christian community at Jerusalem.

VII. THE PRAYER ELEMENT

The next interest which we discover in our material is one which might be considered so general that it would be impossible to discover a situation into which it would not fit, and, therefore, difficult to assign to any particular situation with any high degree of probability. The prayer element in this material emerges first in the eleventh chapter, where we have the shorter and less-known form of the Lord's prayer. The introduction to this prayer is significant: "And it came to pass as he was praying in a certain place, that when he ceased, one of his disciples

[1] Isa. 8:9; Jer. 27:9–10; Mal. 3:5; Exod. 20:7; Lev. 19:26, 31; 20:6; Deut. 18:11. The passage in Deuteronomy forbids any commerce with magic and uses the broadest terms in this connection; cf. "abominations of the nations."

[2] Cf. Deut. 10:20.

said unto him, Lord, teach us to pray, even as John also taught his disciples." This is very Jewish, and to feel the atmosphere one has but to recall the fact that the rabbis sometimes composed prayers for their pupils. This introduction is very different from that which meets us in the Gospel according to Matthew and raises the question as to the situation which may have caused it to be remembered or formulated. It would seem to represent a period in which Christianity had not formulated its prayers and was feeling the need of so doing. Gradually becoming conscious of its difference from Judaism, it would come to feel the inadequacy of the old prayers to meet the new spirit, and thus to lay emphasis on such an element. There is yet another possible indication of the situation: "Even as John also taught his disciples." The persistence of the Johannine movement side by side with Christianity is a fact that cannot be gainsaid. The statement regarding Apollos[1] that he knew only the baptism of John is in point here, while the incident of Paul and the disciples at Ephesus[2] is highly significant. One of the manifest interests of the Fourth Gospel is to combat a persisting Johannine party.[3] The placing of any phase of the Johannine movement in contrast to that of Jesus, as in these introductory verses, indicates a fairly close proximity of the two movements and some emulation.

The continuation of the passage which contains the model prayer[4] deals specifically with this interest. The evident intent of the verses is to encourage the disciples to continuance in prayer even in the face of disheartening obstacles. The basis of encouragement is the fact that they may rely on God to be at least as generous and willing as any human friend. The specific reference to the Holy Spirit as the supreme gift in answer to prayer is very primitive from the standpoint of Christian history.

The second appearance of the prayer interest in our material is in Luke 18:1-14. There are two parts in the passage representing different phases of the matter: (1) the parable of the Indifferent Judge, or better, that of the Importunate Petitioner; (2) the parable of the Pharisee and the Publican. Regarding the first, the evident purpose of the story is to emphasize the necessity and value of persistent, courageous

[1] Acts 18:24 ff.   [2] Acts 19:1-7.

[3] Cf. E. F. Scott, *The Fourth Gospel*, pp. 77-86. As to the continued persistence of Johannine influence in the Sabaeans or Mandaeans found in the Tigris and Euphrates districts, cf. Lightfoot on Colossians, p. 402, and Hastings' *Dictionary of the Bible*, II, 679.

[4] Luke 11:5-13.

prayer, not the unwillingness of God, for the apathy of the judge is but the background of the picture. The seventh verse seems to point to a situation of distress and oppression which calls for the intervention of God. The second phase represents an interest in the control of prayer-custom and habit, and is designed to prevent arrogance and to inculcate the spirit of humility born from a sense of unworthiness.

As we have already stated, the prayer interest is so general that it will be a matter of difficulty to discover indications of special situations which are served by these passages. But we may recall the pre-eminent position which prayer occupied in the early Christian community. The prayer in the upper chamber,[1] attendance at the temple at the hour of prayer,[2] the prayer of the community in special situations,[3] the attitude and practice of the apostles and leaders,[4] and of the laymen[5] demonstrate this with clearness. It was by prayer that the Holy Spirit and its accompanying powers came. This fact alone would be sufficient to show that prayer occupied a place of great prominence. It may be asked: "If this is so, and on the hypothesis that this section represents the needs of the early Christian community, how it is that it does not occupy a larger place in it?" The probable explanation is simple. Prayer was and is one of the most spontaneous expressions of religious life and experience and would not suffer too great a control. One would be justified in expecting that any instruction or guidance in the matter would be general and the touches light. The model prayer of 11:2 ff. would serve to turn the minds of the worshipers to sane and practical subjects, a control so urgent and necessary in a primitive movement, and thus to prevent wild and uncontrolled and dissipated exercise of the activity. Persistence in prayer, especially in the face of apparent failure and hostile forces, would be a subject most apposite; while, on the other hand, persistence in prayer, especially if successful, would easily produce an incipient religious arrogance which the parable of the Pharisee and the Publican would admirably meet. It seems very probable that the need for prayer-control would arise very early in an ecstatic religious community, such as the Jerusalem church was. While the prayer interest of this section cannot be definitely attached to this circle, we can say that it is Palestinian Jewish,[6] and that as far as there are indications of time and place they favor Jerusalem and its Christian community as the place where these traditions took form.

[1] Acts 1:13–14, 24.

[2] Acts 3:1.

[3] Acts 4:23; 12:5.

[4] Acts 6:4; 8:15; 9:40; 11:5; 13:3; 16:16.

[5] Acts 10:2, 30.

[6] Cf. "Went up to the temple to pray."

VIII. THE MIRACLE ELEMENT

We consider now the bearing of the treatment of miracle which appears in this section as evidence for the date and place of the material. The first fact we meet, and it is one of great importance, is that there is but a modicum of the miraculous in the material before us. In 10:3 there is a reference to mighty works which had been done in Chorazin and Bethsaida without any further specification, while none are noted as having been performed in Capernaum, the Galilean headquarters of Jesus. The Seventy are represented as having power to cast out evil spirits.[1] The third reference is in 11:14 ff., where the dumb demon is exorcised. But there is here a distinct impression that the thing done was not a marvelous work. By some the deed is ascribed to co-operation with the prince of demons, while others repudiate it as unworthy of consideration, and request a sign that shall be unmistakably such and bear the stamp of heavenly supernatural power.[2] The miraculous is not by any means here exalted to a place of eminence. Three miracles of healing complete the list: (1) the healing of the woman with a spirit of infirmity[3] (13:10–17); (2) the healing of the dropsical man (14:2); (3) the healing of the ten lepers (17:11–19).

The very modest place which miracle occupies in this section as compared with Mark is striking. In Mark 1—9:29 (the rest of Mark's Gospel is occupied with the journey to Jerusalem and the Passion), that is, during the Galilean activity of Jesus, there are three specific cases of exorcism[4] and five general statements of miracle-working activity[5] in which the impression is given that a large number of miraculous acts were performed, and that they consisted of healings in general and of exorcisms. One of these statements has reference to the activity of the disciples, and it is very significant that, while no limitation is placed on their power to exorcise, their healing activities are dependent on the use of medicinal agents.[6] The Master, however, speaks but the word. Besides this there are eight specific cases of healing miracles by Jesus.[7] In addition to these there is one case of raising the dead[8] and four nature miracles: the calming of the storm;[9] the feeding of the five thousand;[10]

---

[1] 10:17.   [2] Vss. 15, 16.

[3] Note the indefiniteness of the expression πνεῦμα ἀσθενείας.

[4] 1:23 ff.; 5:1 ff.; 7:24 ff.

[5] 1:32, 39; 3:10 ff.; 6:13 ff. (disciples); 6:53–56.

[6] 6:13.   [7] 1:19, 43; 2:3 ff.; 3:1 ff.; 5:25; 7:31 ff.; 8:22; 9:14–29.

[8] 5:21 ff.   [9] 4:35 ff.   [10] 6:33–44.

the walking on the water;[1] and the feeding of the four thousand.[2] How great a weight of the miraculous is here as compared with our Lukan material is very evident. Not only is the miraculous much greater in quantity, but it is heightened in intensity. In Luke the miracles are healings and exorcisms and, with the exception of the healing of the lepers, the cases are left as indefinite as may be. In Mark we have the raising of the dead and the nature miracles. It requires no argument to demonstrate the difference of atmosphere. It may be said that this section is essentially a discourse section and, as such, would not include miracles. It is true that the section is predominantly discourse-material and in so far the objection has force. It is, however, not exclusively so and the predominance has not operated to the exclusion of miracles, as the presence of a few shows.

Passing to the Fourth Gospel we find seven specific miracles: the turning of water into wine at Cana (2:1-11), the healing of the nobleman's son (4:46-54), the healing of the man at Bethesda (5:1-9), the feeding of the multitude (6:1-14), the walking on the water (6:16-21), the restoration of sight to the man blind from his birth (9:1-12), and the raising of Lazarus (11:1-45). Besides these we have definite statements of groups of miracles performed by Jesus. "Now when he was at Jerusalem at the passover, during the feast, many believed on him there, beholding the signs which he did."[3] "The Galileans received him having seen all the things which he did at Jerusalem at the feast."[4] "And a great multitude followed him because they beheld the signs which he did on them that were sick."[5] "His brethren said to him, Depart hence, and go into Judea that thy disciples also may behold thy works which thou doest."[6] "But though he had done so many signs before them yet they believed not on him."[7] Although there are fewer specific miracles than in Mark, the character is similar to those mentioned there, and in some cases it is heightened. The impression is also distinctly conveyed that the exercise of this miraculous power was a very common thing with Jesus and that we have but a few of his deeds recorded. It is to be noticed that the miracle of exorcism has entirely disappeared. Another point in this general review is that in the Lukan section we are discussing there is only one mention of faith in connection with the miraculous and that is after the miracle has been performed and brings an added blessing.[8] In Mark, however, faith is the prerequisite of the blessing which comes through this supernatural power, while in the Fourth Gospel the process

[1] 6:45-52.   [3] 2:23.   [5] 6:2.   [7] 12:37.
[2] 8:1 ff.   [4] 4:4-5.   [6] 7:3.   [8] Luke 17:19.

is reversed and the miracles become signs (σημεῖα) which call forth faith
in the one who performs them.

Let us now examine these data for their interpretation. Entirely
apart from the question of historicity, we find a progress in the matter of
the number of miracles. Between this Lukan material and Mark and the
Fourth Gospel there is a great disparity in this respect. In the character
of the miracles there is also a progress, there being no nature miracles
in the Lukan section, while in the rest of the material they appear.
There is but one specific case of exorcism in Luke and that not highly
favorable, while this type is predominant in Mark and wholly disappears
in the Fourth Gospel. Faith has no intimate connection with the miracles in Luke, it is their prerequisite in Mark, and their result in the
Fourth Gospel. In Mark, Jesus is the constant doer of "mighty
works," which are the outflow of his saving power and are cosmic in significance. In the Fourth Gospel they are "signs" and are evidences of
his person. It is suggested that these data indicate a chronological
development and place this material earlier than Mark. Is this development synchronous with the christological development of the period?[1]
Is it possible that at the beginning the element of miracle was either
ignored or emphasized but little, and that it was only as christological thought became more distinctly formulated and heightened that
this element came into prominence? Moreover, the opposition of
orthodox Jews to anything that savored of commerce with evil spirits
would tend to minimize the emphasis on exorcism. Apart from Mark it
does not appear in any large way. Does its disappearance in the Fourth
Gospel indicate that such deeds did not comport as well with the high
thought of the Christ as did the other miraculous acts? If the sons of
the Pharisees and vagabond Jews did such things they would have little
evidential value for Jesus. The Markan representation comes from a
circle which laid emphasis on these manifestations of power. But while
explaining the silence of the Fourth Gospel on the ground of christological
propriety, we cannot do so in the case of our material. It is much more
probable that an early date is one factor in the minimizing of the miraculous when the future appearance of Jesus as Messiah well-nigh filled the
whole horizon of Christian thought. A later silence would be harder
to explain.[2] Another factor, already suggested, might be found in Jewish suspicion if this material is of Jerusalem origin, for we have already

---

[1] Cf. the discussion of the christological interest, pp. 49 ff.

[2] Cf. Acts, chap. 3, for such a miracle-free representation of Jesus, and Acts, chap.
2, which some think a later phase of thought.

seen that there was probably at Jerusalem a circle which looked askance at exorcism. Thus we reach the hypothesis that the status of the miracle element in this section indicates an early period when the thought of the Christians was centered on other matters and that such a representation comes from Palestinian soil, presumably Jerusalem.[1]

IX. THE STAGE OF CHRISTOLOGICAL DEVELOPMENT AS INDICATIVE OF TIME AND PLACE

Attention must be given to the following allusions to, or statements regarding, the prophetic and teaching function of Jesus. In 10:1 he is represented as about to follow in the steps of his preaching disciples. Although his purpose in so doing is not stated, it is a fair inference that he wished to supplement their message. In 10:25 he is addressed as "Teacher" by one of those learned in the law. The "good part" which Mary chose was receiving the instruction of Jesus.[2] The passage 11:29 ff., where Jesus refuses to give a sign to those asking save the sign of Jonah, places the emphasis on the prophetic message. The way in which Jonah became a sign to the Ninevites was by his preaching,[3] and "as Jonah became a sign to the people of Nineveh so shall the Son of Man be to this generation. . . . . The men of Nineveh . . . . repented at the preaching of Jonah and, behold, a greater than Jonah is here." Thus the sign to that generation was the great message of Jesus. Again, the lawyers address him as "Teacher" in 11:45, and the same title is applied to him in 12:13. His teaching labors are mentioned in 13:10, 22. He is represented in 13:33 as distinctly aligning himself with the prophets. "Nevertheless, I must go on my way to-day and to-morrow, and the day following, for it cannot be that a prophet perish out of Jerusalem." It is quite true that this representation of the preaching-teaching function of Jesus is seen in other material than this, but it receives prominence here. Regarding its appearance in other material it must be granted that emphases remain in vestiges, sometimes frequent vestiges, after a new phase has become the ruling one.

[1] Note the refusal of Jesus to give a sign, Luke 11:29 ff. A most significant change in this tradition appears in the parallel in Matthew, 12:38 ff., where the emphasis is placed, not on the preaching of Jonah, but on his adventure with the great fish. It should be noted that Luke 11:20 makes Jesus say that the finger (power) of God is the agency in exorcism, not Jesus himself by a word, as in Mark. This Lukan representation is in very close alignment with the representation of Acts 2:22.

[2] 10:39, 42.

[3] The Matthean parallel has an entirely different thought.

We turn now to other christological representations. The title "Son of Man" appears in 9:58, but this has no reference other than to the loneliness of Jesus. In 11:30 the title refers to Jesus in his teaching-preaching ministry. If the term as it appears in 12:8–10 is apocalyptic, it is only very moderately so. The eschatological passage 12:35–40 represents the Son of Man as coming. He was not so represented in 12:8–10. It is not, however, the vivid and pictorial eschatology of Mark; it is rather a reserved and indefinite type. A difficult and heterogeneous passage meets us in 17:20–37. Vss. 20–21 seem to be definitely anti-apocalyptic. In the following verses we have a mixture of the apocalyptic and the ethical,[1] but when we compare this with Mark we find that the connection of Jesus (the Son of Man) with the apocalyptic program is much vaguer than in the Second Gospel. There it is "for my name's sake," etc. Thus while the apocalyptic eschatology and Christology appear in this section, the quantity is not great and is very vague in type. The title ὁ κύριος also appears.

The striking christological passage in this section is 10:21–23, in which Jesus, as the text now stands, claims a unique relationship to the Father, a unique knowledge of him, and a unique power to reveal him, which power rests on his own faculty of choice. The discussion of these verses by Harnack in an excursus in *The Sayings of Jesus*[2] is excellent and does much to render intelligible a passage difficult both textually and as to thought-content. As to the Christology, all we need to note here is that the reconstructed passage gives us not a metaphysical relationship of the Father to Jesus, but an ethical one. In the intimacy of this relationship Jesus has gained a great insight into the character of God and is thus enabled to show him to those with whom he comes in contact as no other can. The nature of Jesus is not here a matter of consideration, it is his function and task.

What we have of christological representation in this section does not indicate by any means a high development of thought on the matter. The prophetic preaching phase receives considerable attention, the apocalyptic and messianic side of the question is much less vigorous than in Mark, the title "the Lord" is somewhat in evidence, and the restored form of the famous passage of this section loses its highly developed Christology under the demands of textual criticism.

We now proceed to sketch the various phases of christological thinking in order to find a time and a place into which the phenomena which appear in our material will fit. It must be said at the outset that the

---

[1] Vs. 33.   [2] Harnack, *The Sayings of Jesus*, pp. 272–310.

different phases were probably not sharply distinguished either chrono-logically or as to area. The scantiness of our sources in some quarters renders the task a delicate one, but a general outline may be obtained.

For the early Christians the supreme evidence of the uniqueness of Jesus was the resurrection. It was the ground of their messianic faith, and, if to their Jewish minds the essentials of the messianic task had not been performed by Jesus in his earthly life, they had but to wait for his return on the clouds to see them accomplished. He is "the Christ who hath been appointed for you; Jesus, whom the heavens must receive until the time of restoration of all things."[1] There was a phase of thought which considered that it was first by his resurrection that Jesus became Messiah. The climax of Peter's Pentecostal sermon[2] is in the light of the preceding context best interpreted in this way. The term used is a strong one ($\epsilon\pi o i\eta\sigma\epsilon\nu$). Whatever Paul may have thought of the pre-existence and position of Jesus he certainly considers that by the resurrection Jesus was placed in possession of a more potent messiah-ship than had been his hitherto. On a fair interpretation of Rom. 1:3-4 this conclusion is necessary. In the very nature of the case this adoption-ist idea could not long hold its ground. The future work of the Messiah must be connected with his earthly life. In proportion to the dimming of the hope of his immediate coming was the increase of the demand that his saving ministry appear in the past. Moreover, it is quite possible that unbelieving Jews might ask questions and make statements regard-ing the earthly career of Jesus that would cause no little perplexity and difficulty, and create a need for explanation of the events to which these statements related. That this happened in the case of his death seems very evident from our sources. In the linking of the earthly career of Jesus with his official position and future work what were the lines along which the earthly Christians moved? It would seem that the great mes-sage of Jesus was early taken as evidence of his messianic dignity and work on earth. With the words of Deuteronomy, chap. 18, regarding the prophet like unto Moses whom Yahweh would raise up for his people as a basis and starting-point, the splendid ministry of preaching and prophetic utterance on the part of Jesus could easily be taken as mes-sianic attestation. In fact, this very word is quoted in Peter's sermon as recorded in Acts 3:22, and is there applied to Jesus.[3] Such traditions

---

[1] Acts 3:20-21.   [2] Acts 2:36.

[3] It should be noted in passing that the Samaritans possessing only the Pentateuch would be confined to this representation of the one who was to come.

as the transfiguration would also be pointed out as evidences of a uniqueness on the part of Jesus while on earth. It is quite possible that such
things as the promise[1] of a prophetic person to whose word obedience
was to be rendered, and the exhortation in the transfiguration experience
where Jesus is manifestly superior to Moses, served to meet a problem
which early confronted the Christians by reason of a Jewish challenge
on behalf of the supremacy of Moses. They would perform such a service
excellently. This would appear to be the transition from the attestation
of Jesus by God to a self-attestation.

It cannot be doubted that the early leaders of the Christian community soon found some exceedingly delicate and troublesome problems
on their hands. No sooner was claim of messiahship made for Jesus than
unbelieving Jews pointed out his ignominious death, his obscure lineage,
and lowly origin. In a way that cannot fail to command our admiration
the Christians addressed themselves to their task. The death was
explained on the ground that it was a foreseen matter foreshadowed
by the prophets,[2] that it was in line with the purpose and plan of the
omnipotent God,[3] and that it was for the sins of men.[4] The genealogies
showed his kingly descent and answered the reproach of lowly origin, as
well as brought him into line with the Davidic prince who was to rule.
The supernatural conception explained the entry of this messianic being
into the world. Thus Jesus is Messiah at least from his birth. These
last features, however, were later in making their appearance, however
long they may have been in existence. Between the interpretations of
Jesus just considered is a representation which we find in Mark, where
Jesus is set forth as the user of miraculous power which is employed to
overthrow the kingdom of the evil one. As far as Mark alone is concerned the realization of messianic position and task comes to Jesus at
the time of his baptism when the voice from the heavens declares, "Thou
art my beloved Son, in thee I take pleasure." The temptation story in
Mark and the emphasis on mighty works set forth Jesus as the Messiah
on earth who has conquered Satan and is plundering his domain. Thus
the kingdom of righteousness—the messianic kingdom—has already
begun to triumph over the dominion of darkness and evil.[5] Early the
primitive Christians found strong evidence of Jesus' messiahship in the
saving power which inhered in him and was manifested in miraculous

[1] Deut. 18:18–19.   [2] Acts 3:18.   [3] Acts 2:23.   [4] Cf. Paul, *passim.*

[5] It is interesting to note in this connection the covert note of surprise in the
voice of Jesus, "I was beholding Satan fall as lightning from heaven," Luke 10:18.
This seems earlier than Mark.

display.   This is another self-attestation of Jesus.   When we reach the Fourth Gospel the question has passed beyond controversy—Jesus is the pre-existent divine Logos.[1]

If we have approximated to fact in this meager sketch of the various phases of thought about Jesus as reflected in our sources, it will not be a difficult task to assign our material to its place and date on the basis of its christological ideas.   Two phases appear in the main: (1) that in which the teaching ministry of Jesus predominates, and (2) an eschatological representation quite modified in tone.   Both these phases probably existed side by side in early Christian thinking.   The heralding of Jesus as the Messiah to come could not fail to draw around his person and its interpretation some of the imagery and fancy of apocalypticism. That this was done has been placed beyond question by the Christian Apocalypse which closes the Canon.   The presence of this phenomenon in a modified form in our material argues one of two things: (1) either it has come from a circle which did not approve the type of thought, or (2) it comes from a time when the process was incipient.   The possibility of the prophetic side of the interpretation having arisen to meet Jewish taunts as to Jesus' inferiority to Moses has been suggested above.   These taunts would almost surely arise when Christians began to evangelize the Jews.   Both the phases which appear in this section are Jewish and can hardly have originated on other than Jewish soil.   Where would such thinking and interpretation take its rise?   There is every probability that the early Christian interpretation of Jesus was wrought out by those who had been closest to him in his earthly career.   It was to them the community turned as the fountains of knowledge concerning the church's Lord.   These men for long years had their quarters at Jerusalem and from that point dominated the situation.   It is quite in accord with this that we find both the phases under consideration set forth in the addresses of Peter in Acts, chaps. 2 and 3.   While it is true that the apocalyptic interpretation was not by any means confined to Jewish centers,[2] yet it was Jewish in origin, character, and development, and when probabilities are weighed the likelihood of Jerusalem as its center must be conceded.   As for the prophetic aspect, it is distinctly Jewish, and, both from the standpoint of origin and from that of probable purpose, belongs to Jerusalem, performing its service there in the years

[1] It would be instructive to follow the exaltation of Jesus through patristic literature to the declaration of the Council of Nicea, but that does not belong to this discussion.

[2] Cf. the Epistles to the Corinthians and the Thessalonians.

when the Jewish Christians were pressing the claims of their Lord on their fellow-Jews and meeting their incredulity.

X. THE PROGRESS OF CHRISTIANITY AS INDICATING THE DATE AND PROVENANCE OF THIS MATERIAL

In the well-known passage Luke 10:21–24 we have a reflection of the progress which missionary Christianity had made and was making: "I thank thee, O Father, Lord of heaven and earth, that thou didst hide these things from the wise and understanding and didst reveal them unto babes." It is very evident here that the message of early Christianity had made little appeal and had produced little effect on the intellectual and cultured classes. That this was the condition of affairs in Jerusalem seems to be made abundantly clear by the attitude of the aristocratic Sadducees and high-priestly class.[1] This, too, in spite of the statement that a great company of the priests were obedient to the faith.[2] The cases of the Ethiopian eunuch and the centurion, Cornelius, offer no serious difficulty. The Pharisaic sneer of John 7:48 is possibly a tradition from this earlier time, "Hath any of the rulers believed on him or any of the Pharisees?" That Paul met the same situation and felt the necessity of dealing with it is clear from I Cor. 1:20 ff. There we find that both on Jewish and on Greek soil the response to the Christian appeal has been on the part of the unlettered and unlearned. In that case and in the one before us in the Lukan material the explanation is the same. It is part of the purpose of God; he has called and he has revealed. But we notice that Paul dealt with the question very soon after the problem arose among the Corinthians, and it is but natural to think that the same insistence for an explanation on the part of Jews is met in the section before us. It fits the Jerusalem situation passing well, for that church gives little evidence of possessing leaders or members of the intellectual or cultured type. It is rather strange that the Jerusalem church produced so few men in the course of its history who were at all eminent. As to its poverty and need, the distribution to the widows, the experiment with communism, the request of the council that the poor should be remembered,[3] and the zealous activity of Paul in his collection for the poor of the mother-church[4] leave no room for questioning. Thus this part of our material would fit the situation in Jerusalem and probably in Palestine in all its missionary activities.

[1] Cf. Acts 4:1, 5, 13, "unlearned and ignorant"; 5:17, 24; 7:1.

[2] Acts 6:7.   [3] Gal. 2:10.

[4] I Cor. 16:1 ff.; II Cor., chaps. 8, 9; Rom. 15:25–26; Acts 24:17.

Again, 10:22 ff. seems to reflect a time when considerable work had been done along missionary lines, but when the results appeared rather meager to those who were laboring. Some passages in Acts[1] indicate a marvelous success for the movement from the beginning. But there is strong evidence that the Jews as such steadily refused to give allegiance to the teachings of what was to them an impious sect. It was one of the heaviest burdens which weighed down the heart of Paul that his nation had rejected the Christ and his salvation. It is with no imaginary problem that the apostle is wrestling in Rom., chaps. 9–11; the crushing truth is that the results of the Christian mission among the Jews have been disappointing to a degree. In a similar strain is the lament of the apostle in II Cor. 3:13–16. We have already seen that certain parts of this Lukan material strongly reflect the rejection of the gospel by the Jews. Paul has two solutions: (1) "Their minds were hardened"; (2) the Gentiles profit by the rejection of the Jews, which is but temporary. Here in Luke there is the simpler and less reasoned explanation that this lack of success is due to the providential control of God. Revelation of the truth comes only by the Father and the Son; the disciples are relieved of responsibility when they have faithfully done their part. The early Christian missionaries, in the first blush of their great religious experience, their new belief, and in the face of their inspiring task, could not fail to expect their efforts to be attended with sweeping success. To them their message was the greatest thing in life, in their enthusiasm they could but think that it must compel acceptance with all who heard it. But we know the results fell far below such expectations. Did they turn amid such circumstances to those from whom they had gone forth and to whom they had learned to look for counsel, the apostles, and from them receive this word of the Master to be the answer to their doubts and their encouragement to future efforts? What more probable function could it exercise?

XI. OTHER INDICATIONS AS TO TIME AND PLACE

In the following paragraphs we gather together a few scattered statements which are better treated in this way than by assigning a separate heading to each. The passage in Luke 13:31–35 contains two such. We consider first 13:31–33, in which the Pharisees are represented as advising Jesus to leave the territory ruled over by Herod and seek safety elsewhere, because Herod had designs on his life. It is a curious bit of tradition, (1) because of its fugitive reference to Herod,

[1] 2:5 ff., 41, 47; 4:4, 21; 5:14; 6:7.

(2) because of the very strange representation of the Pharisees as giving friendly counsel to one whom they are otherwise declared to hate and whose life they desire, and (3) because of the vague, indefinite, oracular response of Jesus, dimly suggesting a consciousness that all his course was pre-arranged and determined. It is a weak form of the Johannine "Mine hour is not yet come." It seems to be an isolated scrap of tradition connected here with the following context by the reference to Jerusalem. One cannot avoid wondering how it came to be preserved, especially when it distinctly opposes the hostile representation of the Pharisees. Nor is the statement regarding Herod such as friends of Jesus would care to remember on his lips. Is there an interest which would account for the preservation and use of such a passage? The references to Herod and his followers are sufficiently rare to raise a suspicion that in the mention of these may be found a hint of the solution. In Acts 12:1 ff. we have the statement that Herod the king was persecuting the church, and had gone so far as to kill the apostle James. Then to please the Jews (a fine touch regarding the Herods) he arrested Peter. At such a time when Herod was vexatious to the church the Christians would be interested in remembering any tradition which reflected discredit on the Idumean house, and which would at the same time show that they were but suffering a continuance of the treatment which had been given their Lord. While to our modern way of thinking this might seem puerile, it would have real significance and perform a function of value in a Jerusalem situation. The question also obtrudes itself: If this were Herod Antipas, as it must be in any reference to Jesus, what jurisdiction would he have over Jesus in the neighborhood of Jerusalem? At that time the district of Judea was under direct Roman rule and Jesus had long since left the territory over which Antipas held sway.[1] But it is significant that at the time of the incidents recorded in Acts, chap. 12, Herod Agrippa I was on the throne over the land of Judea. This was the only time a Herod held sway over Judea after 6 A.D. Thus several suggestive lines point to the time when Herod Agrippa was vexing the church in Jerusalem, and the dates of his rule are 41–44 A.D.

Following these verses are two[2] which represent Jesus as lamenting over the city of Jerusalem, bewailing her treatment of those who tried to instruct her, protesting that she herself had rejected all the advances of her Lord, and solemnly declaring that she is abandoned until she shall have acknowledged Jesus as the Sent of Yahweh. When we recall the

[1] 9:51; 13:22.   [2] 13:34–35.

fact that Jerusalem was the scene of the early Christian activity, the birthplace of the church, the headquarters of missionary endeavor for many years, that she remained the center to which the eyes of Jewish and many Greek Christians turned with something akin to reverence for many years more, the preservation of such a tradition is passing strange. If it were in existence and in any way current during those early years it could not fail to give offense. It is in striking contrast to the pacificatory utterances of Peter in his addresses in Acts, chaps. 2 and 3, where he is made to say that the Jews put Jesus to death in ignorance and that they were merely the agents in the execution of the divine purpose. Are there any indications of date or situation in the verses "That killest the prophets and stonest them that are sent unto thee"? Is there any known situation which this fits so well as the death of James at the hand of Herod and the stoning of Stephen? It is a very apt description of two great tragedies which occurred during the early years in Jerusalem. "How often would I have gathered you . . . . , but ye would not! Behold, your house is left unto you desolate! . . . . Ye shall not see me until ye shall say, Blessed is he that cometh in the name of the Lord."[1]

[1] The position has been advanced that the words in 13:34–35 are a late tradition and arose at the time of the abandonment of Jerusalem by the Christians before its fall. I agree with Wellhausen (*Das Evangelium Matthaei*, p. 121) that ὁ οἶκος ὑμῶν does not refer to the temple. It should be noted that the thought of desolation is transferred from the ἔρημος of Matt. 23:38. In Luke it is a simple abandonment (ἀφίεται). Now if this refers to the abandonment of Jews by Christians as an object of missionary endeavor and is at the same time to be referred to about the year 70 A.D. it involves the persistence up to that time of a body of Christians in Jerusalem who were active in the work of propaganda among their compatriots. But whatever facts we have are against such an assumption. After the first dispersion the missionary activity of the Jerusalem church is very small. From the time when James supersedes the apostles in the leadership of the local church that church seems to have lived on terms of friendly toleration with the religious leaders of the Jews. Unless all our traditions regarding James (cf. Paul, Gal. 2:12; Eusebius, *H.E.*, II, 23) are astray, a church under his control would not be likely to develop a situation so acute as that reflected in the sentences under discussion. The removal of the Christians to Pella can hardly be viewed in the light of a missionary abandonment. The personal interest was the deciding one in that case, Eusebius and Epiphanius to the contrary notwithstanding. Moreover, the assumption that later the city will acknowledge the Messiah is not in closest accord with the imminence of destruction which sent the Christians forth. It is more than doubtful if this section would have been connected with the stirring events of 67–70 A.D. had not Matthew brought it into immediate context with the predictions of the destruction of the city. If the Matthean connection be the original it is very hard to find a reason for the isolation of the tradition as it stands in Luke if it is there to be placed in the same historical situation. In themselves the Lukan verses

But the stubborn fact is that for many years after the death of Jesus the efforts of his followers were focused on a city which is here declared to be abandoned. Is it not very probable that this tradition was used to account for and to mark the abandonment of Jerusalem from the standpoint of evangelization, or perhaps the break from the purely Jewish mission? When was Jerusalem so abandoned? The petty opposition of the Jewish leaders and the hostility which culminated against Stephen are set forth in the early chapters of Acts. After the death of Stephen there is the first separation from Jerusalem.[1] The gradual extension of the movement beyond the Jews is reflected in the cases of Philip and the eunuch, Peter and Simon the tanner, Peter and Cornelius, and the first definite work among the Greeks.[2] We find in following the record that this break with the Jewish mission, which was the culmination of a process, took place about the same time as Herod's persecution. This was, as we know, during the years 41–44 A.D. and may very well be the time when our verses found a use. In this connection we must note, whatever our opinion of its trustworthiness, the tradition that a word of the Lord was given the apostles to remain in Jerusalem for twelve years and then go into the world. The form of the statement varies, but the period of twelve years remains fairly constant.[3] The calculation of the year of Peter's death depends on this tradition: $30 + 12 + 25 = 67$. While the forms in which the tradition appears are doubtless apocryphal, yet there may be some foundation in fact for the number 12. On this calculation our verses would represent a Jerusalem situation about 42 A.D.

This same problem of the abandonment of the Jews because of their rejection of the gospel seems to appear again in 13:6–9 in the parable of the Barren Fig Tree with the plea for another year's grace. This would serve well as a protest against a premature acknowledgment of the failure of the Jews to receive the gospel and as a sorrowful admission on the part of the Christians of the justice of their final break with their compatriots. Another phase of the Jewish mission seems to appear in 13:22–30. The paucity of the results of their labors evidently troubled the Christians and the question is plainly put, "Are there few that be

do not refer to a destruction of the city, but to an abandonment. The idea of destruction has been transferred to this by reason of the Matthean juxtaposition of traditions referring to two different events. It seems very clear that these words in Luke are better taken as referring to the missionary abandonment of the city by the apostles.

[1] Acts 8:2.   [2] Acts 11:20 ff.

[3] The Preaching of Peter, *ap.* Clement, *Strom.*, VI, 5, 43; the Acta Petri cum Simone V, and Apollonius, *ap.* Eusebius, *H.E.*, V, 18, 14.

saved?" The answer is a statement of the difficulty of entering the kingdom (which would explain the fewness) and of the need of urgency because of the imminence of the closing of the door. When it is too late and the Jews recognize the superiority of Jesus and his lordship they plead their special advantages—the Jewish idea of favoritism—but this will not avail. Instead of their admittance to the kingdom, those from north and south and east and west, that is, Gentiles, are to have the desired positions. They who were first in choice and opportunity will fail to attain, while those who were considered outcasts are to be the children of the kingdom. This seems to be an eminently apt tradition for the failure of the Jewish mission and the exhortation to urgent haste, as well as the statement that the "wedding shall be furnished with guests" from those who were not "my people." While it is not possible to discriminate sharply, such a situation would probably obtain with some acuteness in the early part of the fifth decade of the first century.

A further interest is that which lays emphasis on almsgiving. Here we are met by that somewhat difficult sixteenth chapter, which, apart from some material which appears to have little or no connection with the main theme of the chapter, is devoted to this subject. The strange parable of the Unjust Steward seems to have its point in vs. 9, the preceding verses being its background and those which follow being in the nature of comment. "Make to yourselves friends of the mammon of unrighteousness;[1] that, when it shall fail, they may receive you into the eternal tabernacles." One immediately recalls the very close connection in a Jewish mind between almsgiving and righteousness. It is evidently an exhortation to the right use of money and would be addressed to those who had possessions.[2] The poverty of the Jerusalem church as well as the Jewish thought of almsgiving would make this a very important question and provide a real reason for the formulation and preservation of such a tradition as this. The section vss. 1–13 manifests an evident purpose to urge almsgiving on those who were able to practice it and to show the superior value of the true riches which cannot be obtained if material wealth is not properly administered. Vss. 10–13 would also comfort the Christians who suffered the privations of poverty. Vss. 14–18 are heterogeneous and break the connection. It is possible that they came in from the margin before Luke got his source. Vs. 19 is the logical sequence of vs. 13 and demonstrates the inability to serve God and mammon as well as the folly of the man who

---

[1] Cf. our "filthy lucre."

[2] Note the exhortation in chap. 11 to the Pharisees to give alms.

has not used his wealth on the basis of the exhortation of vs. 9. As far. as vs. 25 the accompanying thought is that those who experience poverty and hardship now are to be encouraged by the glorious prospect of the future. While this has been a fairly constant Christian appeal. through the centuries, the need for such instruction seems to have been very acute in the poverty-ridden Jerusalem community, and a situation into which this fits admirably is thus found. Vss. 26–31 are not logically connected with the general thought of the chapter. Again we find the troublesome question of the failure of the Jews to accept Jesus as Messiah coming to the front. Does this passage represent the church dealing with the skepticism of the Jews as to the resurrection? In the face of a Jewish taunt to produce the risen Christ, the answer is that a proper reading of the Law and the Prophets would enable them to understand and believe. Such a pronouncement from the father of the faithful could be used with telling force.[1] Again the situation of this appended fragment is Jewish and, with no little degree of probability, Jerusalem.

We have now traversed this material, examining the interests served by it and noting the situations where such interests needed serving. The results have been uniform. Without a single exception the material betrays Palestinian characteristics, and is of a type fitted to serve in situations which are either known by historical statement to have existed there or which can be closely inferred from facts that have strong claims to be considered historical. But we can draw the limits still more closely. Some of the situations which are served by the material here gathered are more easily located in Jerusalem than in any other place. It is indisputable that Jerusalem was at once the headquarters of Judaism and of Christianity, the abiding-place of their leaders, the scene of their first conflicts, and the place where, beyond any other on Palestinian soil, the problems arising from the separation of the Christian movement from orthodox Judaism and the ensuing bitterness would first make themselves felt. Thus, while it is true that some of the interests which seem to be served by this material were not by any means confined to Jerusalem, that city was the place where they first needed serving, and the place where an effort would be made to meet the needs of the growing and expanding organization. The conclusion seems fair that the traditions contained in this section arose in Jerusalem to meet the questions which confronted the Christian community there and to control its development.

[1] In the Fourth Gospel the Jews refuse belief in the presence of one risen from the dead.

As to the date of its crystallization, we have seen that the mission interest is strongly reflected, the Samaritan mission is specifically treated, the question of Pharisaic persecution occupies a place of prominence, the problems concerning the discipleship which would arise very early are faced, and the rejection of the gospel by the Jews and their abandonment as material for evangelization, together with the closely related movement of the Gentile mission, appear. Moreover, the development of christological thought, the progress of evangelization, the reflections on the Herodian family, and other matters give us a more or less defined period in which this material came into use and prominence. Such a period would extend from the martyrdom of Stephen to the acceptance of the Gentile mission—roughly speaking, from 35 A.D. to 50 or 55 A.D.

If these conclusions as to place and time are correct we gain from them a suggestion as to the form of this material which Luke uses. The subjects treated in the material have been noted in the general discussion and it remains only to draw attention to the fact that invariably the questions which lie behind the various paragraphs are questions related to the instruction of the Christian community and the control of the individual and corporate life. The attempts at control are indirect in some cases, but that is entirely in keeping with the situation. The one theological topic of importance, the question of Christology, had in that situation exceedingly practical aspects. There are few things more probable than that leaders who were bearing the "care of all the churches" should feel the need of a manual of ecclesiastical and religious instruction, such as the Old Testament could not afford. It is possible that this block of material, Luke 9: 51—18: 14, formed part or the whole of a primitive gospel document. The topics discussed are distinctly favorable to this hypothesis, while the character of the material, discourse rather than narrative, tends strongly in the same direction. A study of our early Christian literature will place beyond dispute that for a considerable time the only authorities which at all approximated to co-ordination with the Old Testament were the words of Jesus and the declarations of the prophet. Later, much later, appeal was had to the incidents of his life.

Regarding the formation of such a document only the probabilities of speculation are left us. It is possible that the method was in the main agglutinative. A Christian, or group of Christians, possessing a record of a tradition regarding Jesus would actually join it to others when such were obtained. Doubtless the transition from oral to written transmission was very gradual, perhaps spasmodic. Moreover, we are quite familiar with the method of accretion from marginal interpolations. That this material was not deliberately arranged and ordered is supported by the presence of abrupt turns, of breaks in logical connection, and passages evidently interpolated in an earlier combination. This, together with the presence of this material in its present form in the Third Gospel and the convergence of interests and situations upon one period and one place, is an argument in favor of considering this a document from the Jerusalem church. How far it had been reworked before it reached the hand of Luke one cannot say, and the possibility is by no means precluded that the author of the Third Gospel himself left his imprint upon it. But there are a few indications which point in the direction of a composite document, and they are such as to suggest that the material was in approximately its present form when Luke incorporated it. There are two startings for Jerusalem, one at the opening of the section 9:51, and the other in 13:22. Has all the time between 9:51 and 13:22 been spent in Samaria and Judea ? If so, how shall we account for the strange reference to Herod in 13:31 ? A very strange geographical note appears in 17:11, where Jesus is represented as passing along the borders of Samaria and Galilee going to Jerusalem. It is incredible that this is due to the author of our gospel, but is quite comprehensible in a primitive agglutination of documents with the intent to preserve everything about Jesus for practical purposes. There are also two groups of Samaritan material: (1) 9:51–56 and 10:25–37; (2) 17:11–19. The discussion of the question of discipleship appears in more than one place. Other interests might be traced in the same way and would give force to the suggestion that this material as it came into Luke's hand was made up of at least two smaller documents representing similar interests, which documents had been earlier combined into one. The limits of these documents might be given as 9:51—13:21; 13:22—18:14. Within these, again, are suggestions of a composite character, which will not be traced here. But however and whenever this material assumed its present form, it goes back for its first literary formulation to the Christian church at Jerusalem. If a suggestion were to be hazarded it would be that it took literary form when the exigencies of the missionary expansion of Christianity rendered it impossible for all or even the greater part of the adherents to receive the "spoken word" from the "eyewitnesses."

II. AN EXAMINATION OF THE NON-MARKAN MATERIAL CONTAINED IN LUKE, CHAPS. 3-8

The material which forms the basis of our discussion in this section is found in Luke, chaps. 3-8, and includes the following: 3:7-20; 4:1-30; 5:1-11; 6:20-49; 7:1—8:3. It will be observed that this material does not present itself in a compact form, as was the case with the previous section. It is interpolated in the Markan scheme in places which seemed fitting to the evangelist. There are a few coincidences with Mark even in the material we have called non-Markan, e.g., Mark 1:7-8, Luke 3:16; Mark 1:12-13, Luke 4:1-2; Mark 1:14-15, Luke 4:14-15. The first of these is a word of the Baptist regarding the "mightier than I," which might well have stood both in Mark and in the peculiar source, for the parallels are not accurate. The second is an introductory statement to the temptation and has sufficient variation at least to raise the question whether Luke is not here independent of Mark. The third coincidence is a mere transition from the scene of the temptation to Galilee. None of these figures at all seriously in the general problem. Regarding the rest of the material we note that Matthew has some of it almost verbatim, some with more or less divergence, while some is peculiarly Lukan.

A study of this material gives the impression that two, if not three, interests lay back of its formulation and use by the early Christian community. There are two types of material, one being narrative, the other discourse. To one who follows these sections uninterrupted by the Markan basis the difference in type is striking. Any statement as to the bearing of these types and interests on unity or plurality of sources will be postponed until the material has been subjected to an examination.

I. THE SERMON ON THE PLAIN

We shall consider first the discourse-material found in Luke 6:20-49, known as the Sermon on the Plain. The relationship of this sermon to that which appears in the First Gospel will not be directly discussed. The question is a complicated and delicate one and would involve a greater attention to the literary problem than lies within our province. Reasoning a priori it may be regarded as a matter of great likelihood that this quintessence of the teaching of Jesus would assume more than one form and would be in somewhat general circulation. It is generally agreed that Matthew's sermon as we now have it is composite, but we shall follow the question of relation no farther. We pass to notice some facts regarding the Lukan sermon and some interests which appear to be served by it.

As the sermon stands before us in Luke it is manifestly and exclusively a discourse addressed to the community. It is true that in vs. 17 mention is made of a "great multitude of disciples" who are among "a great number of people" who ostensibly hear the sermon, but the address is to the disciples and is direct. It is the disciples who are "ye poor," etc. In the early part of Matthew's sermon the address is indirect and the blessings are pronounced on classes. In Matt. 5:11-12, where the approximation to Luke is close, the direct form of address is used. There is here, however, no suggestion that the blessings and statements have a wider application than to those who are of the inner circle. This points rather definitely in the direction of the early church when the kingdom was the peculiar possession of those who acknowledged Jesus as Messiah and confessed him—in other words, the disciples.

The first section of the sermon, vss. 20-26, deals with the economic and social condition of the community in contrast to that of outside groups. "Blessed are ye poor" is a reference to economic poverty and physical privation. Οἱ πεινῶντες has a physical reference. The general sorrows and griefs of life arising from a variety of causes are covered by οἱ κλαίοντες. The twenty-second verse deals with the question of social ostracism, which developed into contempt and calumny and which had its basis in religious differences. Over against these distressing conditions are set promises which are to be the basis of comfort and the inspiration to duty. To the πτωχοί, destitute economically in a broad sense, the kingdom of God is promised. Whatever may have been the thought of Jesus regarding the kingdom, however ethical and present it was in his teaching, it was a task of no little difficulty to strip the concept of the material and objective in the minds of Christians. While an interpretation of the phrase as indicating their present possession of a spiritual blessing which overcomes the disadvantages of πτωχεία may be possible, it seems much more probable that for the early church there remained in the concept of the kingdom many sensuous phases which were to be a future *quid pro quo* for present discomforts and privations. The supper in the kingdom, the high position of authority and esteem, would serve to extract the sting from present disability. One can easily understand an eschatological turn in ἡ βασιλεία τοῦ θεοῦ. The promises which offset the hungering and mourning look in the same direction. It is hard to avoid the feeling that the satisfaction of χορτασθήσεσθε is physical, and γελάσετε is not the ideal expression for a highly spiritual consolation. The bitterness of social isolation and the burden of slander was to be borne lightly in view of the fact that a great reward was set apart for them, ἐν τῷ οὐρανῷ. But it was ἐν τῷ οὐρανῷ that the Messiah was; from the heavens he was to come to receive them and they were to share his kingdom. So, then, the basis of comfort is participation in the kingdom, prosperity, happiness, and a reward awaiting in heaven.[1] A most unmistakably Jewish touch appears in vs. 23b: "In the same manner did their fathers unto the prophets." One cannot fail to recall at this point the statements of Luke 11:42 ff., where the fathers of the Pharisees and the lawyers are charged with killing the prophets. It is at once evident that this section represents an attempt to console the church in the face of Jewish hostility and oppression.

Vss. 24–26 contain four woes directed against classes which are in straight contrast with the classes of the Christian community mentioned above. The wealth, the luxury, the gaiety, and the social prestige which the opponents of the early church enjoyed must have been a bitter experience and have constituted a serious problem for the church. Only in such a reversal of conditions as is here pictured could the righteousness of God and the value of the kingdom be maintained. That piety must bring prosperity and evil must be punished was the age-long cry of the Jew. By all the nation, save by a few of the élite, these rewards and punishments were thought of in terms of the material. The material thought died hard; in fact, it is not quite without life in modern times. The purely spiritual character of the religion of Jesus, the idea that "virtue is its own reward," were matters of exceedingly slow development. It is not to the discredit of the leaders and preachers of the early church that they appealed by means of the tangible and material. The ascetic element in the verses is in accord with an interest which was discovered in the material considered in the previous chapter. The reference to false prophets is essentially Jewish.[2]

This first section of the sermon reflects the early Christian movement, which is poor, lowly, and persecuted. To offset the discouragement which pressed upon the community the promise of a future happiness already adumbrated is given. The teaching of these verses would meet

[1] It is scarcely necessary to point out how the crudeness and abruptness of these sentences have been softened by Matthew, but a comparison of the Matthean account with that of Luke will serve to emphasize the material and economic aspect.

[2] Cf. Jer., chap. 22; I Kings, chap. 22.

directly the pressing practical need which arose from such a situation, and would also serve as a call to fuller trust and devotion. The poverty and oppression which lie back of these words correspond admirably to what we know of the situation in Jerusalem.

The following paragraph of the sermon, vss. 27–38, deals with the relation of the members of the community to outsiders. The sharp and bitter economical contrast indicated in the Beatitudes and Woes could not fail to tend in the direction of an attitude of harshness and an intense feeling between the two groups, the church and the outsider. Such a situation would require close attention and control. The predominant characteristic of the Christian is to be love and this is to determine his conduct toward his fellow-creatures. Their maledictions and ill treatment are to be met by the Christian virtues of benediction and intercession. Positive opposition to the church and physical injury are to be met by a calm non-resistance, and a spirit of generosity that is beyond expectation is to have free play. No wanton offense is to be given to outsiders, but by all lawful means Christians are to seek to heal the differences. Recognition of the fact that retaliation is the natural thing is implicit, but it would be neither right nor wise. Two motives are urged: a spiritual one and a practical one. The example of the Most High, whose sons they claim to be, should impel them in the right direction. His mercies are toward the unthankful. Moreover, it is a wise policy so to conduct one's self. Non-retaliation and generosity of spirit and treatment will go far to gain for them the desired leniency, and will do much toward disarming their opponents. The principle of vs. 38b is of double application.

This paragraph represents a phase of the disintegration of the old Jewish idea of favoritism. The process required much work as Christianity expanded. It was the first great practical problem, and in many ways the hardest, which primitive Christianity had to solve, and the direction of its solution was to do much to determine the future of the new religion. The words of this section throw a fine light on the continued influence of the profound ethicism of Jesus.

The relation of the members of the community to each other is the subject of vss. 39–45. Attention should be called to the unsuitability of such an address to the disciples in the ostensible situation.[1] Up to this

---

[1] It is quite possible that such an attitude may at some time have been assumed by the disciples. The request of the mother of James and John indicates this. But such could not well have been the case so early as the sermon. Even if it were, is it probable that a tradition so uncomplimentary to the leaders of the movement would have been preserved unless it was of value in a specific situation?

time there has been in the relation of Jesus and his disciples no evidence that any of them are assuming the position of leaders. In any case, that was the very purpose for which he had selected them. But the general attitude of the disciples has been hesitant and timid. In the early community, however, the self-preference of members would be a very probable phenomenon. Those who felt themselves to be in any way superior by position, training, or spiritual gifts would easily assume the position of leaders. Does this question represent a situation when comparative novices are presuming to lead and to teach? Grave dangers would attend such a proceeding. The use of the word κατηρτισμένος indicates their present unequipped condition.[1]

It appears that some of the self-appointed leaders have, from their lofty spiritual height, criticized their brethren and looked at them with contemptuous disapproval. The stubborn fact, however, remains that those who have arrogated to themselves the right to sit in judgment are afflicted with more grievous faults than those whom they condemn. The teaching is very clear that the important matter is the ethical life, not the spectacular and the prominent. That such criticism and such an attitude have become manifest is a sufficient indication of the necessity for a change in the inner life, of which these things are but the expression.

Thus it would appear that under the excellent ethical admonitions of these verses there lies an attempt to meet an exceedingly practical question of polity and conduct. In a new organization scarcely conscious of itself, certainly with no clear apprehension of its full significance, with its various elements requiring care and adjustment, the regulation of impulsive and somewhat arrogant members would be a matter of no small importance. As to the place where such a need would be felt, it is admitted that it would arise in many places, but it is probable that the Jerusalem community early felt the pressure of the problem. There the regularly qualified leaders were present to exercise their authority and control. There also at the time of the disputations in the synagogue of the Libertines and the appointment of the deacons were those "full of the Holy Spirit and of good report" who were forging to the front. In fact, from the time when the gifts of the Holy Spirit began to be manifest there were present factors which could produce the situation which apparently lies behind the admonitions of these verses. Very early in the history of the movement such control as we have here would be needed.

[1] Cf. the problem regarding speaking with tongues and of spiritual gifts with which Paul had to deal, I Cor., chap. 12.

The sermon closes with a section, vss. 46–49, which emphasizes the supremacy of inner religion. The marks of a Christian in the early days were belief and confession.[1] In the first dawn of the movement the fundamental matter was belief in Jesus as the Messiah. Confession was to follow spontaneously. Later, however, under the stress of opposition, confession was emphasized as marking the true Christian. To "witness a good confession" was "a consummation devoutly to be wished." When the attempt was made to compel allegiance to the empire by forcing a confession of the emperor as Lord, more than ever would the confession of Jesus be the mark of a Christian.[2] We shall not be far wrong in claiming that from an early time strong insistence was made upon an oral confession of Jesus as Lord. Under such circumstances the external act could easily incur the danger of being substituted to a greater or less degree for the inner experience. This paragraph makes an excellent corrective for the distorted idea that the naming of Jesus as κύριος has anything essential to do with vital Christianity. The essentials are rather the inner transformation of the life and its control by the principles of Jesus.

The encroachments of externality are so general that it is impossible to state a definite situation out of which alone this corrective would grow. It is, however, scarcely credible that Jerusalem and its Christian community so recently from Judaism and surrounded by strong Judaistic influences could escape this danger.

It is not possible to read this discourse and fail to be impressed by its compact unity. It moves carefully, steadily, and logically from thought to thought and is complete in itself. Moreover, the literary style of the section is deserving of attention. The sermon is composed of sharp, pointed sayings, close, clear contrasts, and moves on steadily from statement to statement to a conclusion. There is balance of thought and expression which is in a measure different from anything else in the gospels. It is not the parallelism of the Hebrew style; rather it is a style affecting the Stoic diatribe. In some parts of the Pauline literature there is an approximation to it.[3]

[1] Luke 12:8; Rom. 10:9–10; Phil. 2:11; I John 4:15.

[2] The story of the martyrdom of Polycarp shows the tenacity of the idea; cf. *The Martyrdom of Polycarp*, ix, x.

[3] The influence of the literary forms of Hellenic philosophic culture on New Testament thought and expression has been investigated only in very recent times. It is natural that the Pauline writings should be the first to come under scrutiny, but there is no guaranty that the other New Testament books have entirely escaped the pervasive

The completeness of the section and the somewhat distinctive literary form suggest that the author of the gospel took an existing source and incorporated it without serious alteration. The perfection of its literary form is evidence for its existence in written form, while the value of its practical suggestions contained in its paragraphs would be sufficient warrant for its preservation in this attractive way. Evidently in its present form we have here a sermon to early Christians. The Jewish touches give clear evidence of its Palestinian origin, while the influence of Stoic literary forms, if accepted, suggests a Hellenistic circle. Of all the Palestinian centers Jerusalem has the greatest claim to consideration, for reasons that are quite obvious.[1] The sermon appears to be the application of the ideas of Jesus to certain church situations which have to a greater or less degree controlled the emphasis. Its isolation in the Lukan Gospel, combined with its literary form and the character of its thought-content, strongly indicates a separate source. It came from a circle not far removed from that from which the Perean material emanated.

II. THE REMAINDER OF THE MATERIAL

We pass now to consider the rest of the peculiarly Lukan material contained in these chapters. The broken and scattered condition of

influence of Hellenism. On the matter of the diatribe, cf. Rud. Bultmann, *Der Stil der Paullnischen Predigt und die kynisch-stoische Diatribe;* P. Wendland, *Die hellenistisch-römische Kultur,* pp. 39 ff.; *Die Literaturformen.*

[1] The combination of an origin on Palestinian soil with the Cynic-Stoic literary tendency may seem to some strange and unnatural. But it is possible that we underrate the Hellenistic influence in some Palestinian centers, especially in Jerusalem. It is true the presence of the temple with its priesthood and its ritual was a strong conservative influence. But the Sadducees who were intrenched there were hospitable to Hellenic culture. It is not likely that the constant intercourse between Jerusalem and Jews of the Dispersion would fail of some influence. The presence of a Hellenistic synagogue, or Hellenistic synagogues, in Jerusalem (Acts 6:8 ff.) is directly in point here. The fact that the members are represented as opposing Stephen does not constitute a serious objection; cf. *Encyc. Bib.,* cols. 4787–88. Stephen himself may have been a Hellenist and have been impregnated with the views and ideas of Hellenism. There were Hellenists in the Jerusalem Christian community (Acts 6:1). Philo is an example of a Hellenist who remained a Jew, but who nevertheless laid under tribute whatever of Greek culture he could use. Josephus might also be cited. With the presence of a body of Hellenists in Jerusalem, with the constant stream of outside influence, and with the characteristic aptitude of the Jews to seize and use the best that other peoples produced, there is no serious reason for refusing to admit the possibility that a Jewish or Hellenistic preacher in Jerusalem might adopt the style which had been so successful in the hands of its exponents. If Paul made use of this Stoic agency our argument is by so much the stronger; cf. Bultmann, *op. cit.*

these sections renders the interests which lie behind them slightly more difficult to recover, but a careful examination will show that there are interests of a dominating character. There are two groups of material which have a common bond in that they relate to John the Baptist, and for convenience here these will be treated together. They are 3:7–20 and 7:18–35.

An early relation of Jesus and John the Baptist seems to be well founded. It is not easy to discover any reason for the production of such a tradition. Its persistence can be due only to its correspondence to actual fact. But in respect to the relation as generally conceived there are some difficulties. There can be little doubt as to the strength and character of the impression which the Baptist made on the people of this country. "They held John as a prophet." In the opinion of the people his office and function was that of a preacher of righteousness. Moreover, we cannot be oblivious of the persistence of the Johannine movement and its possible status as a rival to Christianity.[1] These facts do not quite accord with the representation of this man's gracious withdrawal before the "mightier than I." The early relationship of Jesus and John and the subsequent separation were matters to which the early Christians had to give consideration when they came to adjust their new views of Jesus to his earthly career. The cause of the separation does not belong to our discussion here. The relative positions and tasks of these two great figures were early explained by assigning to John the position of forerunner to the Messiah. Prophecies from various parts of the Old Testament were adduced in support of this claim. This arrangement not only solved the troublesome question of the relationship existing between the movements and their founders, but served to demonstrate and enhance the messianic dignity of Jesus. These are considerations which we must bear in mind as we proceed to an examination of the representation of the Baptist in the material before us.

We are justified in inferring from the paucity of the material that we possess a very small part of the message of John. We must deal, however, with what we have and endeavor to discover the spirit and thought of his preaching. The first thing to be noticed is that John is represented as attempting to disturb that feeling of security in Abrahamic descent which characterized the Jewish people. The lines of nationalism and favoritism are well-nigh obliterated, and an appeal is made to base the life on ethical principles. It is true that there are foregleams of these ideas in the great prophets, but it is surprising to

---

[1] Cf. above, p. 44.

hear this note emerging from an atmosphere of legalism. That, however, is not an insurmountable difficulty. But it is perplexing, on the assumption of its genuineness, to find that no appeal was made to this teaching in the Jewish controversy. Moreover, there appears to have been no opposition to John on the part of the religious leaders. This is indeed strange if he attacked one of their most precious heritages. But since John was *persona grata* to the Jews, a message such as we have here from his lips would be of great value and telling effect in a Christian appeal to Jews who were clinging to their ideas of national favor and covenant privilege.[1] Is there not a subtle and significant reference to the Gentile mission in the words, "God is able of these stones to raise up children unto Abraham"? The situations which the peculiar turn of John's message as here set forth would meet are church situations during the struggle with the Jews over Jewish privilege and Gentile admission.

In vss. 10–14 we have a specific application of the general ethical attitude to various classes. "The multitude" is a term too indefinite to deny to any specific situation. It fits the preaching of John and of the Christian missionaries alike. But the "publicans" as a class yielding to his exhortations strikes the reader as strange. Elsewhere Jesus represents himself as being criticized in strong contrast to John for associating with publicans and sinners.[2] If John came into close contact with them this comparison loses much of its point. However, the possibility is by no means excluded that John's appeals were heeded by them. Little or nothing of such an effect of John's preaching appears in the course of Jesus' ministry. The third class mentioned is the soldiers. Did these go to hear John? Did they yield themselves to a Jewish idea and submit to its control? It is possible, but one cannot fail to wonder if Roman soldiers went to the desert to hear a Jewish fanatic preach.[3] On the other hand, Christianity working in the cities came into contact with, and made appeal to, these very classes. In such an appeal and mission this tradition would be of value. The whole paragraph is, however, little more than a background for the succeeding verses, in which John declares the superiority and announces the judicial function of Jesus. This is the climax of this section and to it the preceding statements are subservient.

[1] Cf. the attitude of Paul to Abrahamic descent, Rom., chap. 4; Gal., chap. 3.

[2] Luke 7:33–35.

[3] That they were Romans, or at least non-Jews, is clear; cf. Schürer, *Geschichte des jüdischen Volkes*, 3 Aufl., I, 459–60; *History of the Jewish People*, Div. I., Vol. II, p. 50.

The other material in which John appears is found in 7:18–35. This section also is difficult by reason of the incorporation of the idea of the forerunner. At the outset there is a lack of confidence on the part of John regarding this personage whom he is supposed to announce. There is genuine wonderment and perplexity. His movement is not merged in that of Jesus, the messengers are still "his disciples." The depressing effect of John's imprisonment is scarcely an adequate explanation for his attitude when compared with other parts of the Baptist tradition. There are but two matters in the section which call for our consideration. The first is the favorable attitude assumed toward the "people" and the "publicans," and the hostile attitude taken toward the religious leaders represented by the "Pharisees and lawyers." Here again we have a reflection of the struggle of the early Christians against the Jewish leaders which was so abundantly manifest in the Perean material. The other matter, and it is by far the more important, is the tribute of Jesus to John the Baptist. Not by any means the least interesting aspect of this tribute is its limitations. With the symbolic answer which Jesus gave to the Baptist's query the incident would naturally be considered ended. But the fact is that the question and its answer are far less significant than that which follows. The words of Jesus constitute a splendid eulogy on the leader of the movement with which he had probably identified himself at the beginning and with which he had broken when he found himself differing from it in thought and aim. John is placed at the very head of prophetic teachers. But with whatever prestige this brought, to which is added that of being the "preparer," John is distinctly shut out from the kingdom of God.[1] Here again the two movements are sharply differentiated. John's position and John's movement are represented as immeasurably inferior to the position of Jesus and his movement.

In this Johannine material two main interests are discoverable. The first is the demonstration of the inferior position occupied by John and the minor importance of his movement as merely preparatory to that of Jesus. This relative position is admitted by John himself according to 3:15–17, and is claimed by Jesus in 7:27, 28b. The chief situation which lies behind this interest is the necessity of dealing with the persistency of the Johannine sect and the endeavor to absorb it in the Christian movement. The second interest is the converse of the former and is an attempt to establish the superiority of Jesus as a person and a

[1] Is the real connection of a Johannine tradition broken by the insertion of vss. 27 and 28b?

religious leader with the corresponding excellence of this movement. This superiority of Jesus is declared by John and is claimed by Jesus. Thus one interest is a question of policy and diplomacy, and the other a theological or polemical one. The diplomacy of the first interest is shown in the generous estimate placed on the person of John the Baptist and the very great importance assigned to his movement as secondary only to that of Jesus. This conciliatory attitude would do much to break down the opposition and prejudice of the members of the Johannine sect. The second interest will receive further attention in the following paragraphs.

We consider now the temptation narrative contained in Luke 4:1-13. This is a distinctly christological section and marks a phase of the adjustment of the facts of Jesus' earthly career to the thoughts which were current in the early church regarding him. The view of the temptation taken by the source which Luke here follows is different from that of Mark, who sees in the conflict of Jesus with Satan amid the beasts a cosmic victory of the Messiah. It is quite true that the Lukan source considers the temptation in the light of a victory over the evil spirits represented by ὁ διάβολος and thereby enhances the figure and personality of Jesus, but that does not exhaust the significance of the narrative. The somewhat detailed discussion of the three temptations serves to explain stubborn facts which seemed to conflict with the messianic dignity of Jesus. The first temptation explains the facts of the economic poverty and humble social position of Jesus. They were the result of a deliberate choice and as such did not invalidate his messianic claim. The second temptation addresses itself to the pressing problem as to why Jesus did not set up a messianic kingdom on earth. Again we find that it was a voluntary renunciation and that such a procedure was deliberately rejected as not in accordance with his plan. The failure of Jesus to reveal himself as a supernatural being endowed with messianic powers was perplexing to many Jewish minds. To give an explanation of this we have the third temptation, in which such a miraculous display as would convince the skeptical is definitely refused. All these questions were difficult and troublesome ones for the early Christians as they pressed the messianic claims of their Lord and were met by the scoffing queries of the Jews. The answer of the temptation story is that all the things which the Jews expected in their messianic king were within the power and grasp of Jesus, but in obedience to a higher ideal and another purpose he had risen superior to their allurements, and was so much greater than any messiah hitherto imagined. Again we have the interest of enhancing the person and official function of Jesus.

At the end of the narrative a word is added which indicates the ubiquitous practical interest of the early church: "And when the devil had completed every temptation he departed from him for a season." This not only shows the completeness of the victory of Jesus over hostile forces and thus serves to demonstrate his superiority to them, but it would be an exceedingly useful word for the encouragement of Christians in the times of stress and testing which were frequent in the early Christian community. It would be heartening to recall that the "head of the church" had been "tempted in all points" and had endured.

The story of the rejection at Nazareth as related in Luke 4:16–30 has likewise a christological interest, although there is a difference in emphasis from the preceding. It represents the mission of Jesus as a preaching one and sets forth his task as that of a prophet. Importance is attached to the announcement of good tidings and the mediation of spiritual blessings. It is the "words of grace" which impress the people, and as a prophetic preacher he makes his appeal to his fellow-townsmen. However, the demonstration of his prophetic mission is not all. He definitely assumes the title of prophet in vs. 24, but in vs. 23 the testimony of his mighty works finds expression.[1] The christological interest of this paragraph, then, has two sides: the supreme message of the blessings of God to men constitutes a credential of Jesus, and the marvelous works which had attended his ministry show his unique power and personality. In our discussion of the development of christological thought in the early church in the preceding section we saw that both these phases had a place.

In the latter part of this narrative the missionary interest issues. The rejection of Jesus at Nazareth has its counterpart in the larger rejection of him by the Jewish people when he is presented to them as their Messiah by the Christians. The two striking instances of the blessing of Israel's God being bestowed on non-Jews in the early prophetic time could be used with telling effect in the struggle of Christianity to

[1] It is possible that vs. 23 may be a Lukan addition to the source under the influence of Mark 6:2. The position of the story of the rejection at Nazareth in Luke is much earlier than that of Mark, who represents Jesus as having done many mighty works in Capernaum before his experience at Nazareth. In Luke, however, apart from 4:23, there is no mention of Capernaum until 4:31, and the writer may have felt it necessary to insert something to approximate the Markan situation. If this view is taken we shall have to modify our statement to the extent that there is but one type of christological representation in this paragraph, namely, the prophetic. But this will in no way affect the argument regarding the whole section.

break the bonds of its early nationalism. This function is so obvious as not to require argument.

The peculiar material of Luke is broken at 4:30 by Markan material, only to be resumed in 5:1. The section 5:1–11 is instructive from our point of approach. The preaching mission of Jesus is reflected in the opening verse, but this is passed by rapidly in order to give attention to another phase of his activity. The interest which centers in the calling of the disciples tends to obscure the important part this section could play in demonstrating the supernatural knowledge of Jesus and his control over natural forces. The accuracy of his knowledge and the immediacy of results impress Simon Peter (the church leader of the early days) with a sense of the uniqueness and superiority of Jesus. The form of apostolic commission which appears here is worthy of notice. This statement of their consecration to a task by Jesus himself and their immediate devotion to it and to his person would be of inestimable value in establishing the position of the apostles as leaders in the church. The point of importance in this paragraph is that it is dominated throughout by christological thought. It sets forth Jesus as the one who has a marvelous and immediate control over both nature and men.

The rest of this peculiarly Lukan material is found in 7:1—8:3 and is strongly marked with a general christological interest. The first part of the chapter concerns itself with the request of a certain centurion that Jesus would heal a servant who was at the point of death. In view of the gospel representation of Jesus as a doer of mighty works there is nothing strange in such a request, but some of the details of the story are very striking. The relations existing between the centurion and the elders of the Jews, the entreaty of the latter to Jesus to respond to the request made, especially taken in comparison with the balder account of Matt. 8:5–13, may suggest an attempt at mediation between the military class, the elders, and the Christians. Much more important, however, is the attitude toward Jesus which the officer is represented as assuming. If a Roman officer showed his respect and esteem to Jesus while Jesus was living it would make excellent apologetic material to the military class in the Christian propaganda. There is here a recognition of the supremacy, the authority, and the dignity of Jesus on the part of this centurion such as is scarcely met with elsewhere in our records. This acknowledgment of these characteristics and its tacit acceptance by Jesus would serve to demonstrate in an excellent manner to any questioning group the right of Jesus to the office and honors claimed for him by the church. It could be used with telling effect with the upper classes. The second striking thing that emerges is the wonderful power of Jesus, whose word is able to heal even at a distance. This unique ability is clearly understood by this suppliant non-Jew. The surprising attitude of the centurion opens the way for the comments of Jesus on the quality and magnitude of the faith exercised toward him. It is superior to anything that has been found among the people who should have been its most noteworthy exponents. This comparison of the faith manifested by Israel and by the Roman fits such a situation as that brought about by the conversion of Cornelius.[1] If this tradition were current at that time, one cannot fail to wonder at the difficulty which Peter experienced in meeting the situation, a difficulty so great as to necessitate a vision. Moreover, how was it that the church so stubbornly resisted the admission of Gentiles in the face of this example of the Master? Is it possible that the tradition crystallized first in such a situation? In this section we find again the twofold interest of showing the superiority of Jesus and of supporting the larger mission of Christianity.

The paragraph containing the narrative of the raising of the son of the widow of Nain has given rise to some discussion. Many hold the opinion that it is a stray tradition inserted here by Luke to justify the statement of vs. 22, "the dead are raised up."[2] It is quite true that it affords a basis for that remark, but it by no means follows that its insertion is due to the author of the Third Gospel. The interest which the paragraph displays is in such harmony with the general interest of the whole chapter, and in fact of the whole of this peculiar material which we are considering here, that there are strong grounds for considering it an integral part of a source which the author is here using. Even if it is to be regarded as incorporated for the purpose above indicated, there is no reason whatever for delaying its insertion till the time of Luke.[3]

---

[1] Acts, chap. 10.

[2] Cf. Johannes Weiss, *Die Schriften des Neuen Testaments*, I, 448-49.

[3] The omission of the story of the raising of the widow's son by Matthew has been thought to be evidence against its being in the source which Luke and Matthew used. This, of course, assumes identity of source for these two writers. Granting this, is there any reason why Matthew should omit it if it were present? He has copied Luke 7:1-10, with the omission of vss. 3-6a, fairly closely in Matt. 8:5-10, 13. The next levy on this source is made in Matt. 11:29, where the question of the Baptist with Jesus' answer and tribute are recorded. In this he follows Luke 7:18-35 with considerable accuracy. But between chaps. 8 and 11 Matthew has recorded the raising of Jairus' daughter, which furnishes a basis for the statement in the reply of Jesus, "the dead are raised up." When we recall that Matthew omits the story of the anointing of Jesus by the penitent woman in the house of Simon, Luke 7:36-50, perhaps because he takes

The alternative is that the author is eclectic and is piecing together traditions as his work progresses. There are very grave difficulties in the way of acceptance of this view.

The incident shows a progress of thought when compared with that of the healing of the centurion's servant, where Jesus is represented as possessing power over disease. Here his power and supremacy are heightened so that he has control of, and power over, death. The ascription to Jesus the Messiah of such a power would leave little to be desired. In this connection it is of interest to note the manner in which Paul grapples with the problem of the relation of the glorified Christ to death and the application of his thought to the resurrection.[1] The effect of this mighty work on the people of Nain is worthy of consideration. It is the prophetic character of the work of Jesus which seems to have impressed them. To them the power and function of this man were those of a divinely sent and controlled prophet. They did not ascribe the power to do the mighty work to the person who stood before them, but to God who had visited his people.[2] As in the other material, we notice here a dominating christological interest.

The question of the Baptist, with the answer and accompanying eulogy of Jesus, has been discussed above, so we pass to a consideration of the incidents of the dinner in the house of the Pharisee.[3] The narrative shows the superiority of Jesus to legal scrupulosity in his refusal to recognize the uncleanness of the touch of the sinful woman. This tradition would be of assistance in emphasizing the authority of Jesus over legal enactments and would help to cut the Gordian knot of the relation of Christianity to the law. It would likewise serve to break down the prejudice of Jewish Christians in working among such people. But these interests are minor ones in this connection. The Pharisee is represented as doubting the prophetic ability of Jesus because of his failure to recognize the character of the woman who anointed him. Jesus appears in the best possible light when he shows not only that he is aware of the

over from Mark 14:3–9 in a later chapter a somewhat similar story, we may conclude that even if he is using an identical source he is not binding himself to an absolute use, but is using selective powers. I am not able to see that the omission of Luke 7:11–17 by Matthew is in any way proof that it was not in the source Luke had before him. The explanation lies in the difference of arrangement of material.

[1] I Thess. 4:13 ff.; I Cor., chap. 15; Rom. 8:1 ff.

[2] Some have seen in several details of this narrative striking similarities to the accounts of the raising of the dead ascribed to Elijah and Elisha in I Kings 7:17–24 and II Kings 4:17–37; cf. Feine, *Eine vorkanonische Überlieferung des Lukas*, p. 40.

[3] Luke 7:36–50.

type of woman who has come to him, but also he is quite cognizant of the thoughts which are passing through the mind of his host. The supernatural knowledge of Jesus is clearly exhibited in the conversation which follows. This is a phase of the superiority of Jesus which constantly characterizes this material. The same christological tendency is seen in the statements regarding the forgiveness of sins. There is no hesitancy on the part of Jesus to pronounce pardon, nor does he appeal to external authority. How great an assumption of official dignity and superiority this was in the eyes of contemporaries is reflected in the surprise of the query, "Who is this that forgiveth sins?" There are practical interests discernible throughout the paragraph, but they contain nothing new and are decidedly secondary to the dominating motive of the exaltation of Jesus to a unique position of power and authority.

The short section 8:1–3 is of an entirely different type and probably does not belong to the source. If it does, it is a vagrant tradition which has attached itself to what was originally a separate document. Its function in the Third Gospel is merely connective. If we should look for an interest which is served by it, it would be found in the communistic or ministrative idea, which would be of value in urging support for those missionaries who devoted themselves to the work of the gospel.

We have now passed in review the material which is peculiar to Luke in these chapters, 3–8, and it remains to gather the main facts and to draw from them their legitimate inferences. We have found imbedded in the sixth chapter what, on grounds of obvious direction, function, and literary style, may be considered a separate written source which the author of the Third Gospel has incorporated practically unchanged in his work. It was probably a sermon, or the digest of a sermon, which appealed so strongly to its hearers and performed such valuable service that it was preserved in this form for wider use. There seems to be justification for the theory that the Sermon on the Plain constituted a separate source for our author. Its date and place of origin are quite similar to those of the material of Luke 9:51—18:14.

When we come to consider the remaining material we are conscious of a different thought-atmosphere, and, in fact, a different literary atmosphere, as well. The discourse-material no longer predominates, but occupies a secondary place to the narrative. The practical interest, in the strict meaning of that phrase, appears only occasionally. In its place we have a controlling theological interest. We have noted the occurrence of a Baptist tradition. This has been brought into alignment with the chief interest of the source, and there is ground for the opinion that a careful combination of literary and historical criticism could restore to us part of a Johannine tradition which did not represent its hero as secondary to Jesus.[1] This does not concern us deeply here, for this Johannine material had been absorbed in the general interest and incorporated in the source before it reached the hand of the author of our gospel. The overwhelming interest of this material has been christological. Throughout its various sections we have detected the purpose of indicating and demonstrating the superiority of Jesus. At one time he is the mighty prophet who by word and deed impresses those who hear his gracious words with a due sense of his unique greatness. At other times he is the supreme Lord over the forces of nature, of life, and of death, as in the healing of the centurion's servant, the raising of the widow's son, the miracles in the presence of John's messengers, and the great draught of fishes. In the realm of knowledge which is beyond ordinary ken he walks serene and undisturbed. His supernatural knowledge enables him to detect the character and hidden thoughts of his fellows, and to be conversant with the secret workings of nature. His control over men is such that a word from him is sufficient to change the course of their lives.[2] Every ascription of superiority, supremacy, or dignity Jesus is made to accept as his right, and, on more than one occasion, actually claims it. It would then appear that what we have here is a document with the definite interest of meeting the difficulties which confronted the early church when it attempted to demonstrate the messianic office, dignity, and power of Jesus while he was on earth. If his failure to meet the requirements of the common messianic ideal was opposed to the claim of his followers, they replied in the story of the temptation that a different purpose involved a voluntary refusal of the exercise of such powers and activities. If his humble and obscure career formed the basis of a taunt or became a stumbling-block to earnest seekers, his splendid message of divine blessing and love as well as his mighty works would be adduced as marks of his personal greatness and demonstrations of his high position. In short, we have here a document which was a christological polemic. To discover its provenance we need only recall the place where the battle for the messianic claims of Jesus

[1] On the whole question of the existence of a document devoted to John the Baptist which has, at least in part, been incorporated in Luke, and on the question of the persistence of a Johannine sect which attempted to rival the Christian movement, cf. Clayton R. Bowen, in the *American Journal of Theology*, XVI, 90–106; cf. also Baldensperger, *Prolog des vierten Evangeliums;* E. F. Scott, *The Fourth Gospel*, pp. 77–86.

[2] Luke 5:10–11.

was first fought. It was in Jerusalem that the apostles first set him forth as Messiah; it was there also that they met with stern opposition from the religious leaders of the people who would have been seriously compromised by any general acceptance of the messianic character of Jesus. Moreover, it was in Jerusalem that, in response to various objections to ascribing this office to Jesus on the part of Jewish opponents who knew the career of Jesus, the first advances in christological thinking were made. If we were right in the sketch of christological development given in a previous section,[1] we are in a position to give a relative date to this document. There we saw that the adoptionist Christology was followed by a phase which gradually thrust the messianic task and dignity back into the earthly career of Jesus and which seized upon various traditions to support its claim. The prophetic aspect of his work, based on the promise of a "prophet like unto Moses," preceded that of Jesus as a doer of messianic mighty works. In the Perean section we found the former representation predominating; here we have both aspects, that of the possessor and wielder of miraculous power being the more prominent. While the impossibility of distinguishing sharply in period between various phases is freely admitted, for there is high probability that different conceptions coexisted, yet a general chronological arrangement may be claimed. So, then, there is reason for placing the crystallization of these traditions and probably their collection into documentary form at that time when the emphasis on "mighty works" was beginning to force the prophetic representation into a secondary place. This would be somewhat later than the material of Luke 9:51—18:14, but earlier than Mark, for in the Second Gospel we have the emphasis on the miraculous highly developed and the annunciation of messianic office to Jesus at his baptism.

Thus our study of this Lukan material has led us to these conclusions: Luke is using at least three sources, besides Mark, in these chapters. There is, first, the material which he has incorporated *en bloc* in 9:51—18:14; second, there is the Sermon on the Plain, which we consider a separate source; and third, there is the christological document scattered throughout chaps. 3, 4, 5, 7. The first and third of these sources are manifestly composite and had doubtless a literary history before they reached the hand of the author of the Third Gospel. They are all Palestinian in origin and the evidence points with some clearness to Jerusalem as the place where they assumed documentary form. Their probable dates have been indicated in the course of the discussion.

[1] Cf. pp. 49 ff.

www.ingramcontent.com/pod-product-compliance
Lightning Source LLC
Chambersburg PA
CBHW062025040426
42447CB00010B/2141